Michael

How
the Real
World
Really
Works

GRADUATING INTO THE REST OF YOUR LIFE

BERKLEY BOOKS, NEW YORK

This is an original publication of The Berkley Publishing Group.

HOW THE REAL WORLD REALLY WORKS

A Berkley Book / published by arrangement with the author

PRINTING HISTORY
Berkley trade paperback edition / May 1997

The Putnam Berkley World Wide Web site address is http://www.berkley.com

ISBN: 0-425-15305-3

BERKLEY®
Berkley Books are published by The Berkley Publishing Group, 200 Madison Avenue, New York, New York 10016.
BERKLEY and the "B" design are trademarks belonging to Berkley Publishing Corporation.

PRINTED IN THE UNITED STATES OF AMERICA

10 9 8 7 6 5 4 3 2 1

Acknowledgments

Several people helped make this book possible. Karen Hauser, Vanessa Drake-Johnson, and Elizabeth Warner offered much-needed wisdom. Denise Dowling's research is appreciated. My editor, Jennifer Lata, gently reigned in my tendency to overdo the smart-aleck one-liners. Helen Merrill has offered encouragement and counsel. Mom and Dad, of course, protected me from the real world for many years, giving me a safety net so I could fall on my face a few times.

This book is for my l'il bro, Steve,
Franklin & Marshall College, Class of '96.
(He's actually rather tall these days.)

Contents

How
the Real
World
Really
Works

chapter one

Getting Paid: Finding a Job

During the summer after my graduation, I had one of those revelatory moments. A passing thunderstorm was soaking New York City, filling the streets with that disgusting gravy that Gotham alone is filthy enough to generate. I'd sought refuge under a restaurant awning, perspiring heavily from the combination of humidity and my wool "interview" suit.

A hand clasped my shoulder. I turned. It was Joshua, a guy from my class at Duke, whom I'd known casually through a couple of classes. He was clad in a fraternity T-shirt, Nike flip-flops, and carefully torn blue jeans. "Dude," he greeted me cheerily, laying on one of those overly firm handshakes.

Joshua gave me the quick update: After a month of "hanging with the fellas down in Freeport," he had landed a Wall Street position that started at 45 grand a year. In contrast, I'd spent six weeks scouring the East Coast for a decent job, my eyes bloodshot from constantly examining the Help Wanted sections. All to no avail.

True, Josh and I had different skills. For example, I could solve complex six-variable equations in under ten minutes. I knew the difference between *perestroika* and *glasnost*. I had a B+ average. Meanwhile, Josh had other skills. He could empty a six-pack in under ten minutes. He probably thought that *glas-*

nost was some sort of streak-free window cleaner. He'd barely escaped with a 2.0 GPA.

But he had been smart enough to call his roommate's mother, a top Wall Street executive, who hooked him up with a no-brainer job where his primary responsibility was entertaining clients—taking them to restaurants, to ball games, to strip clubs; all part of a noble effort to win their accounts.

The point: Forget grades. Forget experience. The process of landing a job has a lot more to do with *(a)* connections and *(b)* a smart, intensive search effort. An entry-level position might have 200 applicants, 100 of whom would be quite competent. So what does the boss look for? After 200 resumes, a 3.5 GPA looks like a 3.2, which blurs into a 2.9. In other words, it doesn't make such a huge difference. A typical moron, like you or me, puts in 5,000 hours over his or her college career to get decent grades. Then he or she shirks on the most important part—turning that degree into a cool job.

This job-hunt thing is not like college, where you apply to two or three schools, have a "safety school," and that's it. You might use up five weeks and 150 résumés just to land a couple of interviews.

After all, over a million people graduate from college each year. That degree, in your parents' day, used to mean an automatic job. Not anymore. If you got a liberal arts degree, you're all too painfully aware that a *lot* of your pals go to grad school not because of any special desire, but because of their failure to find a decent job. Most of those who do enter the workplace are not satisfied with their first jobs. The average stay for a college grad in an entry-level post: nine months. I lasted four months at my first job on Capitol Hill.

Think about it like this: If you put six fulltime weeks into finding work and end up with a job that pays $32,000 instead of $26,000, that's a thousand bucks a week bonus. Not bad.

What Do You Want from Your Job?

Let's go off on a quick tangent. What you want is not the same as what your parents want. Mom and Pop want you to be able to support yourself (meaning a high enough salary to afford a safe apartment, health insurance, and frequent trips home). They want to brag about you to their friends (big-shot corporate trainee beats novelist-cum-waitress any day). They want grandkids ASAP. (Incidentally, prepare for some bitterness when you find that they shower your *kids* with all the toys and presents they never gave *you*.)

In addition, Father (and Mother) might not know best anymore. The last ten years have brought more change to the American workplace than any decade since World War II. You parents know this, but their instinct is still to push you toward a "safe" corporate environment, no matter how many headlines they read of IBM and GM and Boeing laying off thousands of employees.

If you do decide to take on a tough, glamorous, or nontraditional industry—whether it's Teach for America, writing scripts for Comedy Central pilots, or forging rapiers as a blacksmith's apprentice—you definitely want to get the folks on your side. Your actual job will be tough enough as it is, without any emotional baggage from the home front. Mom wants you to be happy. Dad wants you to be happy. They've already accepted that you won't be a doctor (though there's still hope for Junior going to law school . . .), so they might take your decision better than you think. Just don't shove it down their throats.

(Author's note: I had to write the above paragraph for my parents, so, if you would, a grain of salt . . .)

Now, back to that question:

What Do You Want?

It's a tough question. Of course you don't know what you want. That's why you're reading this section, unless you're reading this on behalf of your lazy boyfriend—which means *he* doesn't know what he wants.

The bad news is that there's no easy answer. I'd offer one rule of thumb. If you're torn between two lines of work, with a big salary on one side of the coin, and job satisfaction on the other, go with job satisfaction. Yes, that sounds naïve. But I speak from experience. You'll probably spend half your waking hours at work. Half. If you hate your job, if you are unhappy during half of your waking life, what can you possibly buy that will make the remaining free time so wondrous? What can you possibly own that will please you enough to compensate for 40 or more hours of drudgery every week?

If you're bored by your job, you'll be cranky when you get home from work. Then, down the road, there will be those long nights when you're 37, married, kids, mortgage—stuck—and you fall into the "what if" funk. What if you'd temped by day and sculpted by night? Would your work be at the Museum of Modern Art today?

So whether you're equivocating between paralegal and homeless advocate, or between bond trader and assistant manager of the ballet, go with your passion. If you don't enjoy your work, you're doomed to lifelong misery. And if you *do* love bond trading, more power to you. Can I borrow some money?

What Don't You Want?

If the bad news is that there's no easy answer to "What do you want?", the good news is that, like picking a college, getting your first job isn't as life-determining as it may seem. Remember when you thought that you'd kill yourself if Georgetown didn't accept you? And that by your sophomore year, you realized Georgetown wasn't nearly as important as that? That's how you'll feel about your first job after working for a year or two. You won't be locked into that career forever; there will be plenty of tangents available.

When I graduated from Duke, I desperately wanted a job as assistant to Dr. Isabel Sawhill, who at that time was a senior fellow at a think tank called the Urban Institute. Dr. Sawhill is an expert on the "underclass," a subject that fascinates me, especially topics like inner-city education.

A professor of mine scored me an interview. Talk about your good interviews: I felt like Pacino trying to land a small part off-Broadway, like Jordan trying to win a pickup game. Everything went perfectly.

I didn't get the Urban Institute job, of course, and after a few weeks, I ended up with a "compromise" job. I sat in an office, on the receiving end of a telephone, repeating "Congressman Ackerman's office" about 150 times a day. It was on Capitol Hill, true, but the pay sucked and I'd mastered the phone after only about 45 seconds. So much for gaining job skills. The prospects for advancement were slow—a promotion would come only after a year or so, and the job, "legislative correspondent," basically involved answering letters from constituents.

So I left D.C. and my dreams of fighting urban poverty. I packed my bags to take a job in New York, as an assistant to a theater producer. There I *lived in* urban poverty, but the perks included getting to see almost every play and musical on or off Broadway for free. After a year and a half in that office, I'd learned a ton. But by then the "learning curve" was nearing bottom. Producing is 10 percent strategic decision making and 90 percent repetitive paperwork. I'd wanted to give myself a shot as a full-time playwright, so, once again, I quit my job.

I became a freelance writer, with the idea that I'd make my living writing magazine articles and have lots of time left over for plays. After several months of constant rejection from both magazines and theaters, I got a break. I'd written a few articles for a tiny magazine called *Theater Week,* and an editor from *New York* magazine called me and asked me to write something for him. *New York* magazine was offering ten times the amount that *Theater Week* was offering at that time. In short, I parlayed my very narrow scope of knowledge about the theater business into an assignment for a big magazine. Once I was "in," I could write about other subjects, from basketball to fireworks to . . . urban education.

In other words, it took a few years, but I ended up where I wanted to be. (Dr. Sawhill seemed to do just fine without me, eventually becoming a senior policy expert for the White House.)

What You Want to Get from Your First Job

Your first job could well be in an entirely different field from your ultimate career. However, that doesn't mean that your first taste of the real world doesn't matter. You want to develop marketable skills: how to use various computer software, how to work in teams, how to write reports, how to defuse delicate or hostile situations, and so on. You also want opportunities to prove yourself and to be promoted, so you'll be able to show your future employer a track record.

TO THINK ABOUT . . .

1. What is the future of the industry in which you want to spend your life? You might have dreamed of managing video stores specializing in foreign films, but video stores might eventually become obsolete. Perhaps you've always hankered to be a tax lawyer, but if Congress ever passes a flat tax, you'll be out of business. Being a Broadway composer sounds like a noble aspiration, until you realize that Broadway has decayed to the point where the average season has exactly one new musical, usually either by Andrew Lloyd Webber or Stephen Sondheim. Given the sorry state of the industry, either you'd have to be a once-in-a-generation prodigy or you'd have to sleep with a *lot* of producers to make it on Broadway as a composer.

2. What lifestyle do you want? Do you like to travel, to fly? Are late nights okay? Or did you want to put your all-nighters behind you for good? What about dress codes? Are you willing to wear heels 50 hours a week? Can you bear tying a noose around your neck every day?

Do's and Don't's for Landing Your First Job

DO prove your interest in the field and in the employer. If you have to, lie. Pretend you know exactly what you want. Don't tell the Citibank manager that you'd sell your firstborn to work in commercial banking—and then tell him that you're also considering advertising.

DON'T go off-message. Apply the preceding advice to every communication—letters, interviews, résumés, phone calls. Stick with a very focused message. For example, your résumé needn't be flush with extracurricular activities. If you're looking for a sales job, the fact that you captained the debate team will be impressive and should be featured prominently on your résumé. If you're looking for a customer service position, however, the last thing the boss wants is someone who is skilled in being verbally combative.

DON'T use employment agencies. They tend to specialize either in secretaries or in experienced professionals. You are neither. They'll also steer you to areas which don't interest you.

DO skip the classified ads. This may be hard to believe. But it's just not worth the time and effort to send your résumé only for it to be thrown into a pile of 400 identical ones. Undoubtedly, *someone* will have a connection at any particular office, so if *you* don't, you've got almost no chance.

DO get the Sunday paper from five to ten months ago, if you want to use the classifieds at all. With an old paper, you won't be a fish in a sea of competitors—yours will probably be the only résumé to come that day. Who knows? Maybe that entry-level person is gone. Maybe the boss is unhappy with the person she hired—or happy enough that she wants to promote the original worker, and will thus need someone to take the vacated position. If so, the unpleasant prospect of yet *another* 400 résumés will prompt her to bring you right in for an interview.

DON'T waste your money on the 900 numbers and job-listing guides that claim to have hundreds of job listings. They're almost all rip-offs. As Peter Gabriel says, you've got to "D.I.Y." (That's "Do It Yourself" for any non–Peter Gabriel fans.)

DO take a part-time job while you're looking for a job. It usually takes several weeks to land a job, especially if you're smart enough not to jump at the first one that comes along. A part-time job will earn you cash and help you make contacts (even if the job is not in the field you want, your fellow waiters or cashiers have mothers and fathers, husbands and wives, friends and acquaintances—and *they* might be in the industry you're looking to crack). Part-time work also gives you a sense of self-worth, which is particularly important during this delicate period. It's stunningly depressing to look for a job and gather nothing but rejections.

DON'T pony up for "employment marketing" services, where *you* pay *them* to find *you* a job. The results aren't good. Put yourself in a boss's shoes. Imagine if someone called you, the boss, to find a job for someone else. The whole notion smacks of spoiled bratness or desperation.

DO work as a temp in the field you want to end up in. If you want to become a consultant, find out which temp agency supplies workers to your local Arthur Andersen—and apply at that agency. That way, you can get in through the back door. Once there, by rubbing elbows with actual consultants, you'll not only home-grow your very own network of industry contacts and have the chance to prove yourself, but you'll learn which parts of the business you like (and whether you really want to be a consultant after all).

DON'T mass-mail résumés to personnel departments. Instead, read the trade magazines; nose around the electronic databases like Infotrax and Nexis. Look up various companies; look to find the name of a department head or someone high up. Lots of trade magazines have a column ticking off press releases of people who were just promoted. Maybe the promotion came with an assistant, or maybe the person's old assistant has filled his or her old job, leaving a fresh vacancy for an assistant.

DO try to network on-line. Whether you use America Online or direct providers like Netscape, more and more companies list positions on-line (especially if the job requires someone who is computer-literate). You can also meet people without any imposition. If you want to be a filmmaker, there are appropriate bulletin boards and chat rooms, where you can frankly ask around if anybody is looking for an intern or gofer.

DON'T go to the personnel or human resources office. They'll have plenty of paperwork to keep you busy, but aren't too likely to pull your résumé from the file and call you in for a specific interview—and if they do, you're probably one of dozens of applicants.

DO use e-mail. If you can, get the e-mail addresses of important executives in companies you want to work for. Answering e-mail is incredibly easy for the boss—he or she just jots a few lines and presses Send, without any of the hassles of composing a formal business letter, signing it, finding your address, finding a stamp, mailing it, etc. More important, there are no secretaries to weed out your letters, which means you'll know your letter was actually read (no small feat). Finally, most people respond to each e-mail before moving on to the next one—again because it's so convenient. This means your e-note is much more likely to get a direct response from the head honcho.

Bypassing Personnel

I know a woman—we'll call her Stacy (her real name is Andrea, but she told me not to use it)—who *desperately* wanted to work for network television. She was ready to bribe her way into a job, to sleep her way in, even to take an internship: whatever it took. Her story is short and sweet (and gutsy).

She took a tour of CBS News, the regular walk-through that anyone who wanders in off the street can have. She was dressed in her favorite black Jil Sander pantsuit, and she had a few laser-printed résumés stashed in her bag. As the tour rounded a turn, she slipped off, and walked into an executive-looking office. "Ms. Jackson," Stacy began, having simply read the nameplate outside the room, "I heard there's some reshuffling going on, and I wondered if you were looking for any new blood in the lower echelons of the company." She proffered her résumé aggressively.

"I'm not Ms. Jackson," the woman said. Oh. "How did you get in here, anyway?" Uh-oh.

Well, Stacy had nothing to lose, so she divulged her plan. The executive was impressed. "That's what we used to do in the old days, go plow right in, go get a story. Now we just take phone calls from the press agents and spokespeople, feeding us their various spins." The executive sighed and continued at some length about the decline of television news. Stacy wasn't stupid; she shut up and listened. After several minutes, a very nervous tour guide, accompanied by security, spotted Stacy in the office, but the woman who was not Ms. Jackson waved them off. Stacy got a job, of course: "research assistant," which I believe involves a lot of Lexis searches and some photocopying, but still—she's in.

MORAL: Sometimes your best bet to break into a highly competitive field is to bypass the human resources department—by any means necessary.

DO write and phone companies you want to work for, even if you don't know about any job listed. For this approach, the smaller the company, the better. Midsize firms have the advantage of being large enough to always have openings, but small enough that fewer people come looking. Large firms like NBC, meanwhile, might get a thousand résumés a day, so even if they do have 20 jobs, you're likely to get lost in the shuffle. The only downside to the small and midsize companies is that if you do land a job, they tend to offer fewer benefits. They're also harder to research, which makes it tough to prepare for an interview, should you be fortunate enough to land one in the first place.

How does this direct contact work? After you send the letter or e-mail, give a follow-up call a day or two after they get it. Confidently deliver your pitch, which you should try to keep under ten seconds. For example:

YOU:
It's Mike Goldstein for Oscar Gamble. [First of all, this delivery anticipates "Who is calling?" and also hints that Oscar knows Mike. The secretary may put you through right away, but more likely will say—]

SECRETARY:
Mr. Gamble is busy. Is there a message? What is this in reference to?

YOU:
[Here, you've got to be honest.] I'm Mike Goldstein. I just graduated from Indiana University with honors, I've got some experience, and I want to talk with Mr. Gamble about job opportunities.

SECRETARY:
Sorry, there are no openings. [Here's where everyone else fades out and says "Okay, thanks." But *you* have to be a bit of a jerk and hang in there.]

YOU:
I understand and that's fine; my interest is in discussing the industry with him. I promise I'll be very brief. Please, I'd really appreciate your help. [See, you're not challenging the secretary. You just want to talk to the boss.]

SECRETARY:
Forget it, kid. [She hangs up.]

Well, you can still try with another letter—or five. No one can resist persistence. Send a fresh, short, respectful letter every day for a week, and Gamble's got to give you the time of day. Explain in the letter that you tried to call, that he's obviously very busy, but if he just lets you come in for fifteen minutes . . . Offer to bring him some of the best chocolate-chip cookies he's ever had. Tape a quarter to your letter with a Post-it note stating "The call's on me."

Be prepared for the moment that you get Gamble on the phone. Jot down notes and keep them by the phone, in case he calls. If he does, say "Hi, Mr. Gamble, thanks for calling back. To get to the point, I just finished college—with honors—and I'd like to talk to you about the textbook industry. I worked two summers at Houghton Mifflin, so I've got some experience."

Similarly, if the secretary actually puts one of your phone calls through, then start with:

YOU:
Hi, Mr. Gamble, this is Mike Goldstein. Did you receive my letter? [This is a hook, to engage him.]

GAMBLE:
Yeah, I glanced at the letter, and I wish you the best, but we don't have any openings.

YOU:
I know, that's fine. All I wanted was to come in and talk about the industry, to get an idea of where you think trends are going.

GAMBLE:

What do you mean?

YOU:

For example, do you see textbooks as likely to keep adding multimedia components? My experience with a chemistry textbook was that the software that came with the book didn't work too well. Is multimedia an area that will grow over the next few years? What kind of background do you look for in that arena?

GAMBLE:

Well, strategic planning keeps saying if we don't swim with multimedia, the whole operation sinks. If you ask me, it's just been one giant headache so far. I think it's overrated.

YOU:

There are a lot of worthless multimedia programs floating about. But professors have assigned several CD-ROMS in the past couple years, and some of them are really zippy ones. If you'll just let me come and have a chat, I might be able to give you a customer's perspective on all this techno stuff.

GAMBLE:

You don't give up, do you?

YOU:

Not when I think I'd be a good fit.

GAMBLE:

Let me think about this. I like persistence.

YOU:

I hope this doesn't come across wrong, but I'd love to set up something while I've got you on the phone. I know you're a busy man.

GAMBLE:

Let me check my calendar.

It's worth repeating: Networking is the best, the *best* way to get hired.

Here's an anecdote:

My friends and I used to sit around on Saturday nights, drinking beers and bemoaning that the women always went for guys who were real creeps. Always. We each had at least one "friend," a girl we liked, who was always madly in love with some jerk who treated her like dirt. Then she would pour out her heart to us.

Why couldn't *we* get these girls? Because we were *nice*. We realized that when we came on to girls, some of them wouldn't be interested. Some had boyfriends, some didn't particularly like us. A few actually did think we were cute (we'd learn this years later), and had we ambitiously pursued them, who knows what might have happened? But we never pushed it, because we had no way of knowing whether our advances would be considered romantic or annoying.

Meanwhile, fraternity guys always seemed to score. Why? Besides the status of having Greek letters, they had one secret: Between burps, they came on strong. They were cocky. Sometimes they'd get rejected, sometimes not, but they never seemed to fail to give it the old college try. And I have to give them credit—they often succeeded.

At last, the moral of the story: If you are a decent human being—that is, you like labradors, you don't grab the last slice of pizza without asking, you have sympathy for homeless people—then you hate networking. Make no mistake: Networking means imposing on people. You're being a bit pushy and aggressive. That's not so nice. That's not what you're about.

But since this is *absolutely* the *best* way to go after a job, the *best*, *best*, *best* way, you *have* to do it. Connections are everything in the real world.

Convinced? Once you've committed to networking, the actual execution doesn't require any complicated strategies; you just have to hustle.

Networkers Anonymous—The Twelve-Step Program

1. In addition to talking to friends, family, and neighbors, go to your college alumni office and get the name of every grad who works in your field, as well as every grad who lives in the city where you'd like to end up. If you want to be a copywriter for a New York ad agency, get the contact information for everything from San Francisco ad execs to New York financial analysts. As long as you have a common city *or* a common profession, an alum has a decent chance of knowing someone you could contact about a job.

2. Drop names. "Bruce Wayne suggested I give you a call," you tell the mayor's personnel director. Even if it seems presumptuous, even if you spoke to Bruce Wayne for only two minutes, the validation you get from dropping a name is worth any squeamishness you feel over doing it.

3. Tell anyone you're cold-calling that you just want background information, or an "informational interview," as it's known. You both know that's a lie, but it's a nice way of doing things.

4. If someone stalls and offers to get back to you later, say, "Great. I'm going to be away the next couple of days; may I call you back on Thursday?" That way, you keep the momentum.

5. Be prepared to talk about the industry. Read and absorb the trade press. If you want to break into movies, then you should know that Rob Reiner's company is called Castle Rock; that Seagram's owns Universal Pictures and used to own 15 percent of Warner Brothers; that Spike Lee's next movie is supposed to be a big success.

A Tough Call

Surviving the follow-up call can be a brutal experience. I've always wanted to write for *The Wall Street Journal,* so one day, while I was poking around a writer's group on the Internet, someone gave me the name of an editor there. I immediately sent a cover letter (brief and hilarious, of course) and clips of articles I'd written for *Business Week* and *Money* magazine. Then I called this editor, exactly a week later, to follow up. "Yeah?" he barked. No "Hello." Just "Yeah?"

"Ray?" I began.

"Yeah," he repeated, even meaner this time.

"Um, this is Mike Goldstein. I'm calling to follow up on what I sent you," I blurted out.

He stayed with the monosyllabic approach. "Why?"

I was stunned. "Uh," I mumbled, "why am I following up or why did I send you the stuff in the first place?"

"Both," he said, without a hint of interest.

"Well, er, I, you know, had a few clips, and I was—"

His voice completely changed. "*Oh!* I'm sorry. I'm very sorry," he said, now sounding like an actual human being. "You see, I thought you were a press agent. You gotta understand I *never* pick up the phone. *Never.* But I thought you were someone else. Then I thought I got stuck with a press agent. They're horrible! Oh yeah, I looked at your clips. Good. Yes." I was excited. I waited for him to continue. "We're not hiring. Is that what you wanted to know? Perhaps in a year, if we expand to a weekend edition. Oh. Or did you want to freelance? I'm open to ideas."

Now here was a crushing blow and an opportunity at the same time. They didn't have any staff jobs, but I might be able to sell him an article now and then. I never even knew the *Journal* took freelance writing. So I ended up with something out of the deal.

MORAL: Follow-up phone calls are torturous. You're basically a telemarketer, selling yourself, and we all know the kind of respect we give telemarketers. The best advice is to hang in there, realize that the conversations will likely be awkward, but that you'll have to make the best of it.

Michael A. Goldstein

6. What do you get out of these networking interviews? Info. About the industry, sure, so you'll be able to impress the next person who interviews you. Information about other people you might call. And of course, information about any jobs they suspect might be opening.

7. What do you say to new contacts? Ask about them, personally. What do they like—or not—about their jobs? Where is the industry heading—and how will they adapt? What advice can they give someone looking for entry-level work? They all love to talk about themselves, and will love you for asking.

8. People like to get thank-you notes. Go to an interview with a stamped, addressed envelope and a blank piece of stationery. This is just as important a part of your interview kit as your résumé and polished shoes. You may handwrite this letter, assuming your penmanship is legible. Write the note within an hour of leaving your contact's office. Be brief, but be personal. Drop it into the mail, pronto. Otherwise it might linger on your desk for weeks, buried under some unsuspecting Fritos.

9. Revisit your best leads maybe six weeks later, whether they were actual job interviews or just "informational interviews" within your network. Anybody you had a decent job interview with—even if you didn't get the job—is now part of your network. Milk it.

10. The phone is a great job-hunting tool, but it can be very tough to pick it up. Just do it, whether that means teaming up to alternately make calls with an unemployed friend, or keeping a log to show to your boyfriend—where if you meet your daily goal of 30 calls, you get a half-hour back rub; but if you lose, you give the rub (if not a back rub, something else that's cheap; after all, you're pathetic, unemployed, and destitute).

11. Get names from the newspapers and magazines. When you see a story about the industry you want to work in, look at the names quoted in the paper. Call them up. Focus on names you believe aren't quoted every single day in the paper—if you want to work for the NBA, you wouldn't call the commissioner, David Stern, but you might try Peter Barns, assistant vice-president of marketing. He'll be busy, sure, but he may well be flattered.

12. If all else fails, you can always go to grad school. Or marry someone rich.

Pursuing All Leads

Andrew, a Fordham law student, explains that you have to chase every lead, because you never know which will be the one that will pay off. "I was trying to get a part-time job, a clerkship at a law firm for a few hours a week during the semester. I was discouraged; I'd sent out dozens of résumés, and no one would return my calls. I had worked the previous summer at Legal Aid, so I contacted one of the attorneys there: Did she know anyone in the private sector who might help? She was very discouraging, told me that she only dealt with public interest, blah, blah. Then, kind of under her breath, she said, 'Well I do know this one guy. . . .' I persisted: Who is this guy? Then I wrote him. Of course, when I followed up on the letter, he had no idea who I was. Andrew who? But we got to chatting, and it turned out he needed someone. Right away. Boom, I was in."

MORAL: Don't give up when no one gives you the time of day; the job search is about persistence.

The Résumé

You've read eight billion pages about résumés, so we won't dwell on them here. There are entire books about résumés, when it's really quite straightforward: one page of proofread, laser-printed readable accomplishments (at least 60 percent true) on 20-pound white paper. Don't mess with the fonts or margins to cram more stuff in. Don't use long sentences or blocks. If your résumé were a newspaper, you'd want it to be *USA Today,* not *The Wall Street Journal.* It should emphasize form over substance and be simple enough for a fifth-grader to read—which is likely to be the attention span of whoever is sifting through the stack of résumés.

- Don't list a Job Objective. If your objective is overly specific, you risk not being considered for another job within the same company. If it's too broad, it'll just read like mushy mumbo-jumbo, an instant turnoff.
- Limit personal data to a couple of lines.
- Computer experience is a new must. Call and find out what kind of software the company uses. ("Hi, I'm doing a survey for the Microsoft Corporation. What sort of software does your office use?") Then, list that software on your résumé—if you know it (or at least can fake it). A simple line will do—"Computer Skills: Lotus 1-2-3, Windows, PageMaker, Quark, Quicken, and several other accounting and word-processing programs."
- Stress *results* in the "Work Experience" section. You "cut costs," "increased sales," "were promoted"—in other words, your hard concrete achievements. For example, perhaps you "coordinated voter turnout [that is, you drove a car around] during Congressman Ackerman's reelection campaign. Ackerman won the election, which the November 12, 1994, *Petersburg Daily News* attributed to 'strong turnout efforts.'"
- Don't use ten zillion typefaces. One (something standard, like Times, not Zapf Chancery) is enough. Use bold, italics, and underlining—but use them consistently. If you use boldface for one job title, use bold for them all.
- Keep your cover letter short and sweet.

- Stay on-message. President Clinton is not the Great Communicator that Reagan was. Why not? Clinton knows a hundred times more, and that's the problem. In any one given day, Reagan outlined one or two basic points, such as "We will not compromise our nation's defense" or "I am committed to a tax cut." If a reporter asked Reagan about housing policy on that day, he didn't answer. If someone asked him about whether we should retain the base at Subic Bay, he'd say, "I won't compromise our nation's defense." Simple. So, on the nightly news, editors had no choice; Reagan had said exactly one thing, so that's what they had to show.

  Clinton, by contrast, announces that if health care isn't restructured, we will go bankrupt. That's the message. But then a reporter asks about whether treating cataracts with a new $5-million-per-shot procedure will be retained under Clinton's plan. Clinton explains that as far as he knows, cataract surgery is a laser procedure that would be covered under paragraph 25-b-7, page 143, footnote 5, which will not cover experimental procedures. The headline that night reads: "Clinton's health plan won't cover cataract sufferers." Had he stuck to the basic message, the headline would have been: "Clinton seeks to save nation's health care system."

  The point: Your résumé should cover only a few simple points. During the past year, for example, you interned at *Legal Affairs* magazine and you spent two summers as a paralegal at Broccoli, Spears, and Cheese during college. It's nice that you were president of the Tequila Society and increased membership 200 percent, but that's off-message. On my résumé, I used to try to keep a big section on my tutoring experience, because I figured it would look well rounded—at the expense of spending more space on my more relevant work at the congressman's office. Since then, I've learned to keep a focused message.

A note about lying. Everyone advises not to tell fibbers, that you'll be caught and dismissed. I'm certainly not endorsing lying, but the fact is I know a lot of people who have stretched the truth a bit and weren't caught. You probably won't be caught either. David Geffen told a whopper to his first employer—he said he'd graduated from UCLA, when in fact he had no college degree—to get his start.

Online Job-Hunting

When Dave, a computer science major at Pepperdine, went looking for a job, he didn't buy twenty-pound ivory linen bond paper. "If you're looking for a computer-related job, you can get a leg up using the Internet," he says. "It shows that you practice what you preach."

But geeks aren't the only ones going online to find work. Total listings on the top fifteen online job banks total over 500,000 on any given day. In 1994 that number was only 15,000, so it's clear this trend is accelerating rapidly. Whether you want to be a guitar player, a teacher, a statistician, or a flight attendant, you've got to seriously consider the Internet as a tool.

You can use the Net to find job openings, to chat with others in your desired profession, or to e-mail résumés without any cost, instantly. Job searchers on the Internet require intensive energy, but the early returns show that the success rates can be very high.

Some opportunities and tips for electronic job searches:

- Rather than hunting around a stuffy library, you can often learn about a particular prospective employer by researching their corporate home page. Then act: Type up a quick cover letter, find an e-mail address for their human resources department, and send your résumé out on the spot. No licking envelopes! No looking under the couch for stamps!

- If you do post a résumé on the Internet, use a basic ASCII code. No fancy fonts or indentations—often they won't be legible on someone else's screen. To wow a potential employer, refer them to your Web page, where you can be sure that they'll see the page the way you want them to.
- The Internet is a series of links. Use it as it's intended: take one lead and harness it into several, ask the assistant manager at Proctor & Gamble which you've struck up a correspondence with for some of her colleagues' e-mail addresses. If you're interested in working for a record company, let the web site for Neil Young take you to Warner Brothers records.
- You can enter your résumé in a database where prospective employers search for potential applicants. There's Online Career Center (www.occ.com), the Monsterboard (www.monster.com), and CareerMosaic (www.careermosaic.com)
- Also try an author/consultant named Margaret Reilly (www.jobtak.com/jobguide) and a very general newsgroup called "misc.jobs.misc"
- Check out your rivals' résumés. They're a bit different online, and use nouns more than verbs since they are more likely to fuel keyword searches, i.e., "management" instead of "manage."
- The services above also *list* jobs. There's also CareerPath (www.careerpath.com) which compiles classified ads from many major city newspapers, including the *New York Times* and *Washington Post*.
- In addition to these national job sites, there are several "local" ones, like one for Research Triangle Park near Chapel Hill (www.triangle.jobs).
- You'll have to keep in mind that once posted, you no longer control your résumé. If your boss doesn't know you're looking for something new, this can be dangerous. Here's one solution—post your résumé using "confidential@occ.com" because they have a system where your

name isn't attached to the résumé file. Prospective employers must contact the OCC people if they want you; this acts as a buffer.

- To some extent, enough "old" people (ie., above 30) still think whoever uses the Internet must be really smart. By contacting such executives online, you implicitly take advantage of this misperception. Your IQ is automatically boosted by ten points.
- One study (by the New York outplacement firm Dreake Beam Morin, Inc.) showed that job-hunters using the Internet found more than five leads and one interview each.
- Perhaps the most important element of the online world is its informality. A vice-president who wouldn't think of taking your call or reading your résumé might dash you off a two-line response to an intriguing e-mail. This doesn't mean you can be flip, but you can cut through the "Dear Sir or Madam" stuffiness.
- Don't just look for job openings. Find a "Usenet" group. If you want to be a chef, for example, go where restauranteurs trade tips. Get involved; ask questions; offer ideas; comment on other people's ideas. These are little communities—if you can become a valued member, you can be privvy to an idle remark like, "Our assistant pastry chef was late again today. Geez, you just can't get dedicated help these days." Sound like an opportunity for a quick e-mail?

While You're Looking

If your search is dragging on, or if you're looking in an industry where you don't expect to find a job very easily (such as acting), it's important to have a "day job"—as in "Don't give up your. . . ." A day job is anything that will earn you enough money to buy that StarKist and rigatoni and to pay the rent on the Rubik's cube–sized cubicle you'll call home, all while you're looking for a "real job." Since you're used to a reasonably spartan standard of living and have no family responsibilities, your day job needn't be full-time.

But you must also *beware* the day job! They're especially hazardous if you want to make it in the arts, TV, or some other sexy profession. The most common fate of people with day jobs: They stay with them forever. The dangers are everywhere. A boss who actually likes you. The threat of promotion. A raise. A personnel department that tries to give you health care benefits. Colleagues who respect you. It can happen with day jobs.

There's no rejection, no waiting for agents who won't return phone calls, no galleries who have no use for your sketches, no pain. Plus, a day job still makes you tired. Soon, your auditions are down to once every two weeks. Or you cut out your Friday afternoon voice lesson because that night is *so* busy at the restaurant.

With a day job, you could start earning decent money. You'll get accustomed to the idea of being able to eat dinner with your "real job" friends at restaurants that don't have plastic silverware. Instead of scanning the newspaper for free entertainment—inevitably "The Dogma That Didn't Bark," a poetry reading sponsored by the Pan-African Marxist Kennel Club—you could actually pay the $35 to see Elvis Costello in concert. You might go shopping and blow $110 on a sweater *just for the hell of it*. Decent money can be kind of fun.

So once again: Beware the day job. Don't let it postpone your dream job forever.

THREE IDEAS FOR DAY JOBS

1. **Do-gooder.** Teaching, helping the disadvantaged and the elderly, whatever makes you feel good—all these day jobs help pay the bills, impress future employers, and are personally rewarding as well. Yes, artists are supposed to be cranky, angry, tortured souls, but you don't need your day job to make you that way—get a boyfriend or girlfriend

instead. If you are doing work you actually *like,* you'll have the confidence and positive attitude to push forward with your dream job. And if a rewarding day job takes a bit of the angry, artistic edge away, maybe you can be the fun-loving B-52's instead of Trent Reznor.

Teaching without credentials is not possible at most public schools, but private and religious schools are always looking for people like you. And the new "charter" schools, which are often free to ignore union rules, are also hunting for talented, non-credentialed twenty-somethings. Other teaching options include tutoring, day care and after-school care, SAT prep, spreadsheet instruction, tennis lessons, and the like. You'll have to hustle if you want to find students of your own, but a few weeks of concentrated self-marketing—talking to teachers (at report card time) or tennis pros, putting up signs—can generate some customers.

If you teach in a classroom, however, be prepared to spend many hours working outside of class or you'll get creamed in front of the students. It can also be particularly draining and frustrating, because you'll want to fix every problem, reverse all those years of systemwide neglect, and be a big brother or sister to every kid who comes along.

2. **Temp.** This is the most common way to go. Most important, you determine the hours. If you can type reasonably well, you not only bring home a paycheck, but you also get useful computer experience as well as office interaction, which will familiarize you with the rigors of full-time work. Since a lot of temps are irresponsible slackers, *you* will soon be offered a full-time job by one of the companies you work for when they realize how responsible you are. The allure of benefits and a bigger salary will be tempting, but don't lose sight of your true desire. "If you accept full-time work, your boss will expect you to give up your job search, which means bye-bye to your dream-job

search—whereas temp agencies know you're constantly interviewing and don't mind.

The other upside of temping is that once you prove yourself, the agency might be willing to place you in the field you want to break into.

3. **Server.** This may seem too much like your college summers—waiting tables, tending bar, or doing manual labor to make a buck. But working in a restaurant is actually kind of fun, at least for a while. They feed you. They provide a built-in social world. The turnover is so high that you can land the high-paying Friday and Saturday night shifts reasonably quickly. You don't need experience—if you're willing to lie and tell the manager that you in fact do have it. To apply, just go door-to-door between 2 and 4 P.M. Ask for the manager. Appearance is at least half the battle, so look sharp.

   If you like the sound of "working with your hands," painting, carpentry, resurfacing driveways, and landscaping can all help pay the bills. You can often barter your services for a few classified ads with the local free newspaper and put up flyers in churches and supermarkets to generate some business. If you're any good, the word-of-mouth publicity will kick in.

SUSTAINING YOUR DREAM

Find other people who want to do what you do and form a support group. If you want to be Meryl Streep, the key is to get fellow thespians who desperately *need* to act, not those who kind of want to be actors but have never actually gone on an audition. The latter will actually undermine you because their negativism rubs off easily. Get the aggressive types, who intern with film producers, who bob for gossip, who will give you leads, who will give you feedback, who will help you rub elbows with the successes in your field. Meet regularly.

The Interview

DRESS

There is a lot of blather about what to wear for an interview. But it's really quite simple: Look your best. Fellas, if you have a late-afternoon appointment, try to shave immediately beforehand. Women, don't overdo the makeup, and dress a bit more conservatively if you're interviewing with a woman.

TIME

A lot of people have trouble being on time. It's true. I asked around and heard it over and over. Get it through your skull: An interview is not like meeting your friend Vanessa at 8:00, where it doesn't matter if you get there at 7:55 or 8:05. Be early—not on time, *early*—and be prepared to wait. Have something to read. If there's any company literature lying around, grab that first. Otherwise, bring a book—preferably one with a title that could open a conversation and play right into your hands.

PERSONALITY

It's your presentation more than your actual answers that matter. They'll size up your maturity. They want to know if you'll be fun to hang around with, whether you'll bitch and moan about cleaning the coffeemaker, whether you can play shortstop on the company softball team. They'll decide if you can work well with Andrew, the brilliant but wildly impatient accountant. So you should be so incredibly positive that you're almost embarrassed inside.

Interviews are not fun for interviewers either. Nine chances out of ten they'll never see you again, so it's kind of a drag from their point of view. And remember: As cliché as your answers seem to you, their questions seem to them. So you have to provide enough enthusiasm for two.

NAMES

Focus on remembering names. You need to say your interviewer's name with confidence. Repeat it at the beginning if it's foreign or difficult to pronounce, and use it during the first few minutes of the conversation.

STAY COOL

You'll be confronted by failings in your résumé; suck it up. Obviously, don't blame the professor, even when it was his or her fault. We've all been screwed; just don't mention it, because no one wants to hear it. The correct answer is: "My 3.2 average is really two GPAs: the socially confused me during my freshman and sophomore years, when I drank a Valdez's worth of beers and pulled in a C average; and the me you see before you now—I got a 3.5 during my junior and senior years, in addition to taking over the campus debate team and leading it to a regional championship." See? No excuses. No blaming. Just healthy self-promotion. (Of course, you might want to tone down the Valdez bit.)

Sometimes interviewers are jerks. I had an all-day interview with a corporate research firm in northern Virginia. The morning was great. But after lunch, some guy came in, and *asshole* is the only way to describe him. We did a mock phone call: I role-played trying to ask the president of a fictitious company about sales figures. But my interviewer was brushing me off, not giving me a chance to even finish my sentences. I got pretty angry. Still, after I finished with this loser, the rest of the day was terrific. But I didn't get the job.

A year later, I ran into Dawn, another Duke grad, who was now working for this same corporate research firm. I asked her if that asshole still worked there, or if he'd been indicted for molesting farm animals. "Oh, he's a great guy," she told me. "That part of the interview is called 'The Hot Seat.' They try to get you all ruffled and see how you react."

Oh.

Since then, I've learned that you may get very uncomfortable questions, just to see if you can remain composed under pressure. I'd pulled a Bill Buckner (the infamous Red Sox first baseman whose critical error cost his team the 1986 World Series) and choked.

An Anecdote

Randall, a 1996 graduate of the University of Virginia, tells about a bad interview experience. "I had interned at a prominent investment bank during the summer, so when I got back to school, I tried to stay in touch about being hired when I graduated. Finally, I lined up an interview through the human resources department. This was around Thanksgiving, so I had to make special plans to come to New York, just for a shot at this bank. So I walk in the door for my 11 A.M. appointment, wearing my very best—and only—suit, and knock on 'Vera's' office door. 'Can I help you?' she asked. It turned out no one had told her that I was supposed to interview with her. She was willing to talk with me, but was obviously busy and a certain, um, less-than-enthusiastic tone had been established. I did not get hired, not surprisingly."

MORAL: Always call the day before to confirm your interview.

Interview Questions

To questions that start "Would you be willing . . .", your answer should be automatically *yes*, whether the rest of the sentence is "to travel abroad?" or "work sixteen hours a day, no weekends, with a half hour off for Christmas?" Say *yes* now.

Hang in there. Later in the game is the time for any reconsidering. For example, let's say an assistant manager does preliminary screening, then the manager does the finalists. If the manager really likes you as a finalist, the "travel abroad" thing may not loom so large.

A common mistake is to hide from your potential employer that you're looking at competitors. If you're up for a job at MCA Records and you're asked where else you are looking, feel free to say that you're pursuing jobs at Warner and Atlantic. Package yourself as a hot commodity. Don't B.S. this one, though—if you tell the guy at Roy Rogers that you're applying at Burger King, too, he might say, "Oh yeah? I used to work there. Who's your interview with?"

EIGHT COMMON QUESTIONS

1. Tell me about yourself.

2. Why didn't you get better grades?

3. What are your strengths and weaknesses?

4. Tell me about [the first job listed on your résumé]. What were your responsibilities? What was your boss like?

5. If you want to be in banking, why did you major in political science?

6. Do you plan to go to grad school?

7. What do you see yourself doing in ten years?

8. Why do you want to work for us? In this industry?

TURNING THE TABLES

When the interviewer asks, "Do you have any questions?" say *yes*. Three to five questions is about right, and this phase should last at least five minutes. Don't ask about salary or fringe benefits, not yet. If you're absolutely sure you want this job, you can be aggressive—"I would love this job. What's the next step in the selection process?" If you go this route, be prepared to pay or play—if they make you an offer, you can't stall with, "I think I'll take it, but I gotta talk to my parents first."

Ask questions that show your knowledge of the firm. "I understand that you have developed a new bean burrito with the Rolaids mixed right in. How do you plan to market it?"

Underscore your interest in advancing within the company. What position follows entry level? What happened to my predecessor? Promoted? Terminated? Quit?

FOLLOW UP

Write and mail the follow-up thank-you letter the *same* day. Keep it short and personal: The first paragraph should be about the interview, the second about your top two qualifications. A full week after sending that letter, you can call to follow up.

THE OFFER

The hardest thing to do, especially for a first job, is to negotiate. But remember, they liked you *best*. They want you *most*. They will not take away an offer if you ask for more, as long as you're reasonable, though they certainly might turn your request down. You might say, "I definitely want to work at Calvin Klein, Inc., but I have college loans to repay. Is there any way you'd consider $50 more per week?" (Notice the phrasing—you still have plenty of room to accept the job even if you don't get more money. And by giving the figure as "$50 per week," it sounds much better than $2,500 per year.)

When you get an offer, here's what to think about:

1. Compensation: salary, overtime, bonus.

2. Career progression and date of first review. This is more important than salary. If you can prove yourself in six months and get a raise, you may be better off than you would be if you took a job that starts out paying $2,000 more per year off the bat, but doesn't give you a review for an entire year.

3. Medical benefits. (To compare a job with benefits to one without, just subtract $3,000—or whatever it will cost you to buy your own coverage—from the salary of the job that does not offer the insurance.)

4. Vacation.

5. Start date.

chapter two

Getting Paid More: Keeping a Job

O kay, so you got a job. That was the easy part. The tough part is excelling. What follows are some hints for surviving the first few months . . . and beyond.

Training

On your first day, you may be in for a surprise. Here you are, wearing your finest duds, ready to apply your brilliant analytical skill to restructuring the company. You're ready to dive in. Then some guy from human resources spends your entire first day teaching you how to operate voice mail, the company phone system, the e-mail system, and the like. "Oh, please," you think. "I've been doing all this stuff for years, and even if I do run into trouble, I can always look through the manual."

This is not an uncommon feeling. Your boss has a name for those new hires who are overcome by it—"resistant trainees." The information is either obvious, rote, or so dry that you can't absorb it, so you space out.

Even worse, there are those diversity and sexual harassment seminars, which you probably will look at as a waste of time. And you're probably right—most companies cynically offer this training for legal or PR reasons. "They're telling us all about how our investment bank is doing so much to promote diversity," said one of my friends, who works for a major Wall Street investment bank. "Then you look around the room, and there's precisely one African American, one Asian, and one woman in a room of 25 trainees."

For any sort of job training, you may not actually learn much, but you've got to keep up a good appearance. Let your superiors think they've done their duty—expect the training to be boring, but pay attention and get off on the right foot. You may even be pleasantly surprised.

Speaking

The office climate today is a strange one. In some environments, vicious, obvious sexual harassment abounds. In others, light banter can be wrenched out of context and used against you. One of my friends, Jill, worked for an executive recruitment firm. After she had successfully dodged several overt passes by her boss, he literally showed up at her apartment on 68th Street in Manhattan, parked out front with a dozen roses. The sad reality was that she knew that if she chose to complain, the company's president would back her boss—they had started the company together and had been friends since college.

Could Jill have sued or filed a complaint with the equal opportunity agencies within the state or city government? Sure. But she was scared, didn't want to get wrapped up in the fight, and needed the cash. She just put up with it.

Another friend, Lenin, is a textbook editor for a major publisher. He dated a co-worker for about a year, until she dumped him. Later, after she was denied a promotion, she decided that Lenin (who wasn't even her superior) was to blame, and concocted an absolutely false harassment charge against him. She also secretly recorded a phone call he made to her, and led him into making some mildly damaging remarks, which she excerpted and replayed for the company's president and attorney.

They took the claim seriously, and Lenin was hauled in to address the charge. Ultimately, he was vindicated, but not without an incredible amount of stress and fear.

The bottom line is that humor remains a necessary part of office life on one hand, yet downright dangerous on the other. The rare Demi Moore *Disclosure* situations notwithstanding, women are generally the victims of actual harassment. But men can occasionally fall prey to oversensitive accusers as well.

I don't mean to trump up the reverse discrimination thing. The pseudofeminists who insist that *tomboy* become *rough-and-tumble child,* or that a fourteen-year-old girl be called a woman, aren't taken very seriously in most offices. Meanwhile, plenty of Bob Packwoods and Clarence Thomases continue to prey on women, especially young, unmarried ones. Real sexual harassment of women, you'll find, remains a big problem, despite all the media attention in recent years.

But certainly, during your first few months on the job, err on the conservative side. Keep quiet, keep your romantic aspirations to yourself, and learn the rules of engagement in your office. Both men and women should certainly try to avoid dating in the office—it's hard, because you meet so many people—rather than subject themselves to the risk of future trouble.

What to Wear

It's sad, but true: For your first few years in an office, you should not try to make fashion statements. For many a recent graduate—yes, you—the problem is that for the last four years you flipped-flopped to "work" every day in faded Levi's and that threadbare AC/DC T-shirt (circa 1979). So you're tempted to dress like your most casual co-worker, when you actually should err on the side of copying the most conservative employee. Often, one or two people in the office make a habit of flashy dress; don't get sucked in. Older hands may be cut some slack when they saunter around in fire-red dresses, bold chalk-

"I used to have an entire closetful of high-powered Liz Claiborne and Harve Benard suits," says Margo Connors, a salesperson for IBM, a company legendary for its unspoken, uptight dress code—until 1995. The company had lost billions of dollars over the last couple of years: Gen X hackers in Tevas and Batman T-shirts had invaded the industry, to the point where it seemed like the only people who *didn't* know anything about computers were the ones wearing ties and heels. So in an effort to shake up the troops, IBM's chairman relaxed the button-up rules.

Connors was overjoyed. "I literally banished those suits from my closet," she says. "No more pearls, no big gold earrings. Now I wear a Swatch rather than my gold Seiko, flats instead of heels, khakis and a polo shirt or a long cotton dress with white canvas Keds." Connors had previously owned just suits and jeans, nothing in between. "God, I must have spent a thousand dollars over the last few months on slacks and jackets. But I save half an hour every morning—less ironing, less hairstyling, less makeup, less *hell*."

Another dress code note comes from Emily, 25, who used to be a page for a network studio. "It was uniform hell," she says. "You wear this navy blazer, a white oxford, a tan skirt, and this retarded burgundy tie—all of which they provide." The company provides just one blazer and one skirt, and "after a while, the smell gets rough." So Emily hopped over to do production work at MTV, where "basically, there is no dress code. Every day is a casual day. Today, a woman wore knee-high boots and a tiny skirt, with her hair in pigtails. No one said a word. And when you're on location, forget it. I worked at MTV's Beach house the last two summers, and two Band-Aids and a string are plenty."

Sallie Merritt Green was director of marketing development at *Time* magazine in New York, and prior to that was the marketing director for *Buzz* magazine in Los Angeles. She talks about regional differences in dress. "In L.A.," she says, "formal clothing was never a factor. But back in New York, your professional perception is definitely affected by the way you dress."

stripe suits, blue jeans, or micro-mini skirts. Not you. Even if your boss says she doesn't mind, your fellow drones may become resentful. Plus, you're young, so conservative attire *might* help hide the fact that you're inexperienced, prone to major mistakes, and likely to one day give 45 minutes' notice before quitting and setting out on a six-month cross-country road trip.

Simplicity is the rule for corporate attire. Simple, isn't it? Assuming you're not laboring among Cobain-ettes at a laid-back, sneakers-only computer software maker, you know that grays, blacks, and blues are the building blocks for a business wardrobe. (Note that cheap navy-blue clothes tend to *look* cheap—they get sort of shiny after a few months.)

The trap, though, is a relatively new creature: the dress-down Friday. More and more companies offer a few days when you're excused from the unspoken uniform, and this is where young employees screw up. Play it safe. Keep your Air Jordans and white canvas Keds at home; wear loafers or flats. If only a few people wear jeans, stick with your khakis. If everyone is wearing jeans, then okay, wear yours, but don't pick the pair with the hole in the knee (I know, I know, you didn't cut the hole to be fashionable, the pants ripped on their own).

Accepting Criticism

They might call it *feedback,* they might call it *comment,* but you know what it really is: criticism. It can be hard to take. You're used to college, where B is the typical grade, where failure is rare. Welcome to the real world. To succeed, you'll have to learn how to harness criticism, rather than flip out (a more common and instinctive reaction). Here are a few tips:

1. Even when someone is angry at you, stay cool. Don't wilt. Don't counterattack. If you manage to remain civil and professional, you'll not only allow the person to vent (which means ultimately you won't have to actually *do* as much to satisfy him or her), and you'll gain the upper hand

because once your critic's rage has subsided, he or she may well be embarrassed.

2. If someone is criticizing you in front of an audience, cut him off. "Thanks for mentioning that, but could we discuss it later, alone?" (Now, however, you're implicitly criticizing him—he might get defensive but will probably agree anyway.)

3. Remember: The critics are almost always *partially* right. At least. And the truth hurts. So expect to have an emotional gut reaction, then override it.

4. Listen. Don't think of what you'll say in response. The more you let her talk and seem to acknowledge her concerns, the less *action* she'll want to see on your behalf.

5. Paraphrase his complaints. The office is not a courtroom. Don't immediately cross-examine his points. By repeating his beefs, you'll earn his gratitude, because he knows you're listening.

6. Here's where you can take two paths when dealing with critics:

   a. Ninety percent of the time, they're right, and you should assume that you will benefit from positively reacting to some portion of their criticism. If they're at least partly right, then:

      • Ask "action" questions, like "What can I do to keep the files better maintained?"
      • Commit to at least one action.
      • Figure out how you will make sure the change lasts.

   b. If they're wrong, and you don't want to modify your behavior, then paraphrase their complaint; say "I see your point," and promise to get back to them in a specific, short amount of time (anywhere from five minutes to 24 hours). This sends a signal that they are being taken seriously, even if you plan to disagree with them directly. It also gives you some time to let the sting go away and think rationally; perhaps you'll change your mind and realize they have a point. Finally, by not confronting them directly, you'll have a chance, later, to twist their words a bit and insert your own solution into their words.

Here's an example. I'd finished a long essay for *New York* magazine about fixing the Broadway theater industry. The man assigned to edit the article was new at the magazine. "It's way too long," he said. "We'll have to start by cutting your last two sections, and then—"

I cut him off. "First, it's exactly the length that my contract says. Second, if you cut the last two parts, you'll undermine the whole premise—without them, we'll get all these letters to the editor saying I'm a union-basher without any constructive ideas. Third, the way it works around here is that you have to go to bat for me with the editor-in-chief; otherwise they'll cut it to nothing."

This was a bad way to handle criticism. For starters, my essay *was* too long. Not only had the editor-in-chief already decided my piece would be trimmed extensively, not only had this new editor already stuck up for me by arguing to have it cut by 50 percent instead of 60 percent, but the fact was that the average reader of that magazine simply would not wade through an 8,000-word article.

Second, I was acting defensively without listening. I didn't give him a chance to outline his constructive ideas of *how* to cut. It was like Al Gore telling the president that we need to cut federal spending, and Clinton cutting him off before he even heard any of the ideas.

Third, this editor thought I was a twit, which I was. As a result, the process was a tense one.

Are there better ways to handle criticism?

Yes. Obviously, I should have started by hearing the guy out. For example, I could have taken notes, not only to make sure I got his views, but to send an unmistakable signal that I was taking him seriously. I should have acknowledged his premise: Yes, we have to cut. I should have asked more questions: "What did you think was the essence of the essay? What were its most entertaining parts?" Then I should have proposed action: "Why don't I sit down with those two sections and other parts and see what other big chunks we might slash. Then let's you and I go through this thing, line by line, and trim the fat."

Office Politics

Your co-workers are, in many ways, like your classmates. There's the hard worker, the brown-noser, and the super-aggressive jerk who will even stoop to sabotage (like hiding reference books in the library so no one else can find them).

Some career manuals advise you to stay out of office politics. Yeah, right. The reality is that you'll need to deal with office politics and the various cliques, or people will run all over you. Certainly, you needn't become a Nixonian political animal, drawing up enemies lists and eavesdropping. But unlike school, where tests and papers allow merit to clearly shine through, the workplace often values how well you publicize your success rather than the success alone. You also must work in teams sometimes, so it's important that you end up with other capable individuals.

How can you get office politics to work for you? First of all, you need access to at least two networks of co-workers. The *advice network* is where you can turn to learn how to get things done. The *trust network* is where all the juicy gossip is floated.

In other words, if you just put your nose to the grindstone and don't keep your antenna up, you may well be screwed. Some colleague might claim your success. The best example in recent history is Roman Cortines, the chancellor of the New York City public school system. Cortines didn't want to play politics in what was, by definition, a very political job. As a result he was always being undermined in the media by Mayor Rudy Giuliani. The most egregious claim came at the end of the 1995 school year, when for the first time in memory, reading and math scores had rocketed. Giuliani, who had in fact slashed the education budget as mayor, actually tried to claim credit for the progress, when it was Cortines who had clearly put the successful reforms into place.

It's not enough anymore just to do your job well. My father is a metallurgical engineer; he's been with the same company for 30 years—and your father probably has, too. As you're well aware by now, the era of working for one company that employs you from ages 25 to 65 is gone. Not fading—gone. My dad is always worried about his job security, no matter how productive he is. The conventional wisdoms of even ten years ago are obsolete. So to succeed in the nineties and beyond, you'll need to be a part-time office politician.

Why? Office politics used to be driven by ambition. But with the nineties trend toward layoffs, politics is more a function of fear. From 1984 to 1994, IBM, AT&T, and GM laid off 240,000 employees. If your boss had to let someone go, would it be you?

Again, for the record, most career counselors advise "staying above the fray." But, in my opinion, that's bull. Appeasement didn't work for France and England 60 years ago, and it probably won't work for you now. If a rival starts spreading lies, challenge her directly, then go to the boss. If a rival tries to undermine your report, challenge him on *his* report. Make it clear that for every hostile action, there will be an equal and opposite reaction. You'll probably convince the rival to stop it. However, you do risk escalating tensions, as well as making the boss angry at both of you. Still, I say if someone wants to play hardball, grab your bat.

So if a co-worker acts surprised when you do a good job, don't just take it. Ask, "Why does it surprise you when my work is well done?" If he steals your idea, don't let it happen again. Don't share ideas out loud anymore; send out a memo and "cc" it to the boss. Or use a line like, "An excellent idea, as I suggested to you last week." If she remarks that your project could have been better, let her know you'd appreciate her input while the work is in progress.

Confront gossip when it concerns you. Say what really happened directly to the person you suspect of spreading the rumor. Don't be accusatory, just state the facts. "I heard somebody talking about my meeting with the boss, and I wanted to make it clear what we talked about. . . ."

If a co-worker is merely annoying, you have to put up with some of it. Just keep it to a minimum. Never ask a whiner, "How are you doing?" That way, she won't have an opening. Let her be miserable alone.

But don't let someone off the hook who doesn't pull his weight. Put him on notice: "This project is ready to go and your part isn't ready. When can I tell the boss that this will be done?" The next step, if necessary, is going to the boss and explaining, "The project is finished except for one step (that is, your co-worker's)—in the meantime, what do I do next?"

If an equal tries to give you orders, confront her, even though it will probably make you uncomfortable. "I'm not sure I understand your role in the office," is a decent beginning.

The National Association of Working Women has the "Job Survival Hotline," 800-522-0925, for workplace questions on office politics, harassment, glass ceilings, and so on.

Other Survival Skills for the Office

1. Scan the Help Wanted ads every few weeks. Is your company hiring? Are its rivals? Get a feel for the marketplace; it'll help you with everything from getting a raise to transferring to the hot division.

2. Keep in touch with the consultants, customers, and people from other companies with whom you have contact. They

may be valuable later, especially if you want to change jobs from a position of strength (that is, while you still have one). That way, you won't reek of desperation. If you are unlucky enough to be handed a pink slip (actually, the slips are usually white), you'll soon find that you can fit your workplace "friends" in a phone booth—and Superman won't be there, either.

3. Find out what's happening in other departments. If you work at a bank as a loan officer, ask what's happening in new accounts. After all, they may be launching a major drive to land new customers, which would mean the bank would soon have more money for you to lend. That, in turn, might mean an opening for a new loan manager. Why not start angling for the position early? Then again, if your pal on the corporate side mentions that the board of directors is pushing to cut back on their risk position, you might read the writing on the wall and start checking out other banks for openings.

4. Are you generally reluctant to criticize? Most people are, including most bosses. In the old days, the saying was, "No news means good news"; in today's workplace, "no news" means only that you're not trying very hard to get news. Ask for feedback from your boss and your colleagues on everything you do. Don't wait for that annual review—talk to your boss at least every two months for his opinion of your performance. Not "Hey, Mr. Roper, how do you think I'm doing?" He might well answer, "Fine," and be done with you. Schedule an appointment, go out for a sandwich, whatever—just make sure you get very specific comments. You may well learn that something you've been busting your butt on is not very important to him—but that another task you've let slide is high on *his* agenda.

5. If you want to give constructive criticism, speak up—with caution. Sometimes the veteran employees have been close

to a situation for so long that they've lost their perspective. Don't assume that other people have already thought of and rejected your idea. Your initiative will often be appreciated.

6. When it comes to gossip, listen (and enjoy), but don't put out, at least not too much. Remember that many rumors turn out to be false, and you may never know which ones were true. When you do gossip, try to steer clear of talking about your boss; at least co-workers can't hurt you directly. Also, don't confuse put-downs with gossip; gossip is information (sometimes damaging) that you trade, while bad-mouthing doesn't provide any news, just opinions. In other words, slamming a co-worker can't help but *can* hurt.

7. Your company and job *will* change. Anticipate it. When that continuing education brochure comes in the mailbox—I know, you still owe $7,500 to the University of Texas, but don't chuck it right away. Scan for any practical courses, perhaps in finance, computers, or other technology. You may not need new skills for your current job, but then again, you *will* one day leave your current employer, whether voluntarily or through more persuasive methods. Your boss might well agree to pay or share the tuition costs for appropriate continuing education.

What If Your Boss Is a Pain in the Neck?

Somebody has to be in charge. Fine. But why is it so often someone who is indecisive, insecure, insufferable, or incompetent? As you gain experience in the workplace, you'll realize that some people who were as friendly and reasonable as Dolly Parton when they were colleagues turn into Leona Helmsley (the Queen of Mean) once they are promoted above you.

Some bosses don't put the company first and don't believe that by communicating better with you they'll improve your productivity. They may not even be experts in their field, just experts in acquiring power. To them, you're not necessarily an asset, and you might even be a threat. If you do excellent work, they might lose you to another division or another company, or you might even one day pass them in the ranks.

Shaky managers can be classified into a few categories (and if you are anyone's boss, even an intern's, look for yourself in these categories, too):

- Loners. They're smart and superconfident, and want to do everything themselves. As boss, they'll entrust you with no more than menial tasks.
- Losers. They're wimpy and negative, always worrying about failure rather than pursuing success. They will nix your innovations, avoid risks, and look to cover their own behinds.
- Bureaucrats. A subset of Losers. They invoke official directives and rules (rather, *some* rules—others they'll ignore when convenient) toward whatever goal they have—which is often avoiding any extra work.
- Egomaniacs. They have to have the last word. They don't often spare the whip with serfs like you—certainly not with those who have the audacity to challenge their opinions.
- Smoothies. They'll throw little treats your way, compliment you, confide in you about the lazy bum down the hall—then give the lazy bum the same flattery massage, with you as the new "bum."

If your boss is a Loner, dream up projects that you'd like to pursue, then ask—in writing—for those projects. Loners realize that you need work to do, so if you make it easy for them, you can end up with some plum assignments. Also, find out what kind of work they hate, then jump on it. You'll become indispensable, and have leverage to grab some meatier projects in the future.

If you work for a Loser or Bureaucrat, hold his hand. Show how you can protect him from the risks he perceives.

There's no straightforward way to deal with Smoothies or Egomaniacs. To some extent, you have to say what you think she wants to hear. An Egomaniac needs to be stroked, of course, but a Smoothie often does not. Beware of awards and title changes, which the Smoothie might use to get you to take on additional responsibilities without a raise.

Remember that your boss has a boss, too. The big boss has quirks of her own. So your boss might behave in what seems to you to be a stupid way, but may make perfect sense given *his* boss's expectations.

Directly Challenging Your Boss

Sometimes a policy is flat-out wrong, and there's no way to dance around it. When you feel a need to walk into the lion's den to challenge a policy, remember a few pointers:

1. Briefly cite the policy in question, then pump the plus side of your alternative first. Show your boss how it will benefit *him,* by making him look better, saving him money, and so on. Somehow weave in how one of his ideas was the genesis for your proposal.

2. Next, make the case against the current policy. This has to be powerful. Come up with some way of explaining away each element of the policy as being beyond your boss's control. That way, she won't feel attacked.

3. Quickly push on to anticipated objections to your alternative. Again, try to credit him at every level.

4. Go back to the current policy: Tell what you believe will happen if it remains in place. Again, put all downsides in his terms—how it will hurt the way *he* is perceived.

5. Don't beg.

6. Don't attack.

7. Repeat a few times that you're on his side.

8. Use graphics, if possible. This is a campaign, just like a presidential election—Paul Tsongas might have had a much better deficit-cutting plan than Ross Perot, but Perot had all those zippy charts. For some reason, graphics seem to *validate* new ideas.

Working Late Nights

It's common for employees to work late, even if they aren't compensated. Some jobs simply can't be done in eight hours. Others are prone to crisis. Sometimes the work environment can be so hectic or so filled with meetings that early morning or late night is the only time available for true concentration.

But often, the late nights have nothing to do with productivity. Some people have husbands and wives they loathe. Sometimes they have a boss who works late, and are afraid to leave before her, even if their tasks are complete. A workplace where late nights become common is self-perpetuating: No one wants to be known as the lazy one who won't put in time, so employees go at three-quarters speed during the day, spreading out nine hours of work over twelve hours.

How to escape this unpaid overtime routine? Come up with a regular 7:00 P.M. (or whatever time) escape hatch that your boss approves. Classes are always the best; clubs are okay as well. If your typical routine is an after-work jog that you always seem to shelve to stay at the office, join a running group. Wait for a day when you finish a particularly tough or successful project, then use the short-term leverage to mention your new activity to your boss and even ask permission (maybe invite him to come, too, if you know he doesn't like to run). Talk up your new activity around the office, so no one will question where you are all those nights.

1. **Be a team player.** You've got to see the whole company picture. Have lunch with people from other departments, volunteer to help other employees. If you volunteer, you'll be seen as a go-getter and be able to control your own destiny.

2. **Find a mentor.** You need guidance to move through the ranks, and a special relationship with a senior employee is a great help. The obvious benefit is that if he or she is promoted, you might come along for the ride. Often you have to take the first step and make your interest in being mentored known. A few would-be mentors might be too busy or too lazy to help you, but most people like having a protégé.

3. **Don't panic.** Perhaps you were assigned to do a two-week report tracking the impact of the latest ad campaign on sales. After eight days of wrestling with Lotus, you realize that you screwed up entirely and you'd be better off starting from scratch. What do you do?

   Here's what you *don't* do: don't walk into the boss's office and hyperventilate, blaming the computer (the file was deleted!), the software, your sick dog, or the incompetent intern who was supposed to enter all the data. Instead, give the basics—and *only* the basics—of the problem, then propose your solution.

   Did you catch that? Your *solution*. If you know what went wrong, the solution may simply be to ask for an extra week. If you're still struggling, the solution may be, "I spoke with Charlie, the systems analyst, and he agreed to help design the basic setup." The boss just wants to get this thing resolved. As long as you address the problem straight-up, she'll be satisfied. Perhaps Charlie will do; perhaps next week is too late; perhaps the report was a low priority, something to keep you busy, and now your boss has an important assignment for you.

4. **Perform.** It sounds so simple: Customers want service. Personal service. A human voice, a live body, which makes them feel valued. Courtesy, in many cases, is more important than product quality. Au Bon Pain, a growing fast-food chain, has spread across this nation like a virus. Want to know why? Sure, the food's not bad. If you eat there reasonably often, however, you'll notice that you recognize the employees, and they may even recognize you. Why is that such a big deal? Because at most fast-food joints, employees tend to last just over ten minutes. Au Bon Pain retains workers more than twice as long as its competitors—because it pays more—which means the customer is less likely to get a trainee bungling the order and more likely to get a hello.

Getting a Raise

Remember, you're at the point in your life when you can be most aggressive. Push hard. One, you can survive even if you cross the line and you're fired. When you're 40 and have three kids, you lose a lot of this leverage. Two, you're not making that much. If you push to make your $25,000 salary into $30,000, it's not going to break the company. When the 50-year-old senior manager wants a boost, however, she might be looking to make her $210,000 into $250,000, and that's a big chunk of change for anyone.

Here are a few scenarios to watch out for:

1. **The Dodge.** You don't get your tiny annual bonus until right before Christmas—and then your boss has already left for the holiday. She knows your anger will subside over the holidays.

   What to do: Write a memo, letting your anger spill out

in all its molten glory. That way, you won't be a grinch to your family over Christmas. Then, on January 2, write a new memo without any of the four-letter words and hand-deliver it to the boss. "I wasn't happy with my bonus. Do you have a moment now to discuss it, or could I leave this memo for you to read?"

2. **Home Court Advantage.** It works for Shaquille O'Neal and the Los Angeles Lakers; it works for a boss. He's sitting behind the desk, perhaps making notes, armed with all sorts of distractions. You sit exposed, hands in your lap.

   What to do: Take notes. This will underscore your "I mean business" attitude, make him a bit wary of his vague promises, and help limit your defenseless posture.

3. **Being on the Defensive.** It's not usually malicious, but bosses have been known to pick a time when you're more vulnerable to criticism. Using a completely hypothetical example which never could happen in real life, suppose your superior at Philip Morris calls for your review just three days after you muffed that Virginia Slims ad—accidentally sending *Time* magazine a spoof with a mustache drawn onto the photo of a beaming model. (She's *certainly* come a long way, baby.) "Listen, Mike, this kind of stuff is going to get us both fired. I'm trying to cover for you, but things are going to have to improve. I'm putting myself on the line for you, and I know you've got the talent, but don't you think I should expect more?" Last week you would have replied, "Boss, look at the record sales on Barbie Thins [the cigarette for kids]! My work speaks for itself." But this week you're on the defensive, muttering that the Virginia Slims goof will never happen again.

   What to do: Stall. Tell her—on her terms—why your schedule is so busy you couldn't possibly talk until late next week, since you're focused on several projects which will make her look good.

4. **The Form Letter.** Some companies send an identical letter to the entire staff, giving everyone the same percentage raise, even when you've been led to believe you'd get a *personal* review. Your boss refers you to the human resources department, who refer you to the president, whom you dare not disturb.

   What to do: If your boss got the same raise as everyone else, he's probably ticked off, too, so recruit him to your side. Don't treat him as the enemy. Try to get a personal review by telling him that you want to take a thorough look at your strengths and weaknesses. Go through the process, state your case, and ask if your boss will recommend to his superior that you be given a bonus. If not, ask for extra vacation, an IRA contribution, tickets for the company's luxury box for Miami Dolphins games—any perk you can reasonably request.

5. **The Rushed Review.** "Let's make this quick, because I've got that sales meeting in ten minutes." Or, "Hold that thought for a second, I've got to take this one call." You get the picture. Not only will you feel pressed to cut your presentation, but your rhythm will be shaken. "As I was saying" is not a good way to lead into an argument, because all your forward momentum has been defused.

   What to do: Tell her you have several things to discuss with her, that it's obviously an inconvenient time, that you have an assignment to finish (name something she'll consider important). Ask her if you can buy her a cup of coffee in a few hours, that you'll come by at 4:30 and get her.

6. **The Blame Transfer.** It goes something like this: "Jennifer, you've been doing an absolutely fantastic job, but as you are well aware, those bastards on the ninth floor just aren't allowing me to pay you what you deserve." If you protest, he'll say, "Christ, I'm going to bat for you, I had to fight to get the salary you did get, even to save your job. You know the cost-cutting that's going on around here.

Those bastards are crazy not to give a talented young person like yourself what you deserve, but I hope you're aware I'm doing everything I can to get you more."

What to do: Persist. Use your accomplishment list, and be aggressive about claiming credit for your work—about what you've done for your boss. Remember, most of us were brought up by our parents not to ask for too much and to be grateful for what we have. Pressing for a raise, then, instinctively feels like "bad behavior" and will make you feel awkward. Just hang in there.

Getting That Raise: It Really Happened

Heather had worked for three years at one of those huge pharmaceutical companies that gouge us customers on prices for prescription drugs (she still works there, so we'll call her Heather Locklear for now), and was moving up the ladder. "I'd had two raises, true, but whenever they brought in someone new from outside the company, the new hire would start at a higher salary than mine. I had to snoop around to find this out, which probably wasn't so ethical, but I suppose you could say I had reasonable grounds for suspicion." The point was, she wanted a sizable raise. First she tried the direct approach: She asked for one. "My boss told me we were cutting back, that our division was underperforming, and basically pushed me aside. I was afraid to press the issue. But I found myself getting so pissed off over the next few weeks, I knew I had to do something. So I went back to him, and asked: 'What can I do over the next year to better serve you and the company?' We made some goals and I wrote them down, right in front of him. The subtext was clear but it wasn't like I was shoving it down his throat." The result? After nine months, a month before Christmas bonuses, she walked back into her boss's office to review her progress—and brought along that piece of paper. "I got a raise that was bigger than my first two combined," she says.

7. **The Empty-Pocket Syndrome.** The most common evasion to granting a raise, of course, is the old "Times are tough. Wait till things get better, and we'll take care of you as best we can." This is insidious in a couple of ways. First, it's an appeal to your loyalty: a "don't kick us when we're down" subtext. Second, unless there's a very specific, short-term reason why profits are down—you're a stock analyst and the market just crashed—there's a good chance that things won't get better anytime soon. Third, if things do pick up, you and your boss may not agree on what constitutes "being taken care of."

Your boss might combine the empty-pocket tactic with offering a sweet new moniker for your business card— "Senior Associate" instead of "Assistant," for example— but no *dinero*.

What to do: It may be true. The company may have no money and your boss may be forgoing a raise as well. If so, you'll have a tough time making a case. But don't let this sometimes-valid excuse slide so easily. Is the owner or top management taking a pay cut? After all, they'll benefit in a big way from an upturn in the business's performance— so they should have to shoulder more of the hard times. Your boss may not earn a raise *per se,* but she might get extra compensation: vacation time, a cash bonus, additional health benefits. You can press for similar nonsalary remuneration.

Again, play to your strengths. Make your case by stating that, true, the company's earnings may be down 20 percent, but they'd be down even *more* if you hadn't done *x,y,* and *z.* You understand that times are tough, blah, blah, blah, but you feel that your contribution was exceptional, and you took the job expecting to prove yourself and be rewarded. You might ask for a deferred raise, pending some specific improvement in the company's fortunes. That is, you might ask for a deferred $100-a-week raise, and if Bob's Burritos hits $10,000 a week in sales within twenty weeks, you get the $2,000 (20 weeks x $100) retroactively.

Now that you know what to look out for, how do you get your cash? Make a plan. Decide in advance what you want, how you'll state your case, and what your backup tactics will be.

WHAT DO YOU WANT?

Well, there's the money, of course. But dream up a "wish list," too, with any perks you'd like. Health benefits, a 401(k), a new chair, better lighting, your very own office, an intern or secretary, a company credit card, an expense account, extra vacation days, one Friday off per month to do long-range planning, and so on. Present these to your boss as a series of necessities—which will ultimately benefit him in your increased productivity—not as a laundry list of demands or whimsical desires.

This gives you a broad front of negotiating points, so your boss has room to make concessions. And if he won't move on the most important request—salary—then you might make it up with, say, an extra week of vacation. With three weeks off instead of two, you could even temp for a few days and pick up an extra few hundred dollars—which ultimately equals a bonus.

HOW DO YOU PREPARE YOUR CASE?

First, make sure you have a face-to-face review. Sometimes reviews are done as memos—and you can't negotiate with paper.

Next, before the appointment, send a short written accomplishment list. No comments. No demands. No conclusions. No trumping up your work. Just facts. "For your convenience in our upcoming review, I've written up how I see my accomplishments this year. . . ." Head off criticisms. Acknowledge your mistakes, too, projects that didn't work out, then take responsibility for them. The list works in two ways. One, the boss is put on alert that you will not be easily brushed aside. Two, it's a sort of résumé, presenting yourself in the best possible light. Three, you'll have a starting point for your discussions. Bring a copy of the list to the meeting; within the first few minutes, produce it and ask your boss if he thought it was accurate.

Rehearse. Marshal all your facts and figures, then do a practice pitch to a cranky friend who can try to shoot down your contentions.

HOW DO YOU STATE YOUR CASE?

Once you're face to face with your boss, open the dialogue by steering toward a positive topic. Start her talking about something she'll like—a big account she just landed (with your invaluable help).

Remember, each one of your points must be presented as a benefit to your boss; that if you're happy, if your desires are fulfilled, you'll be a more productive worker who makes her look good and lightens her workload.

Don't make the first concession. Obviously, your unspoken threat is if you don't get what you want, you'll either look for another job or allow your performance to drop. Of course there are ten thousand people who could replace you, but that means your boss must train yet another employee. Does she have time for that—again, so soon?

Don't get carried away by the emotion of the moment. If you're unsatisfied, don't give an ultimatum! Wait. Go home. Can you get another (better) job? Wouldn't it be better to look from the security of your current job? Can you get another offer as leverage to keep your old job—but get that raise?

A point of wisdom: If you feel exploited, you'll hate your job—even if you like the actual tasks, you'll resent the company. Many people go through life like this. You know them. Their bitterness inevitably spills into their personal lives. If

How the Real World Really Works

55

you're not happy and not appreciated, plan to leave. *But* take at least three months of searching for a new job while sticking out your old one. Use your vacation time and make a big effort. I've had friends who bailed out from jobs they hated—then all their contacts dried up and they couldn't find new jobs.

What If You're the Boss?

The day will come when you become a boss. Maybe it's a promotion, complete with a cool title for your business card, an extra $150 a week, and a staff to manage. Or perhaps it's just that an intern has been assigned to you. Whichever the case, you must realize that your life has changed big-time, and that it's easy to turn into the boss you always loathed.

Employees are investments. Some freshly promoted managers treat their charges like gold—if the price goes up, great; if not, too bad. These bosses hope to land a quality employee who will perform well, but feel they can't influence the performance very much. Other bosses treat employees like a stock portfolio, investing time and energy to personally affect the overall productivity. Which type of manager are you?

DELEGATE

The key, of course, is delegating. You can tap into your employees' talents, lighten your own workload, motivate by entrusting important assignments, promote teamwork, and if need be, provide yourself a scapegoat. But what most people don't understand is that you have to invest time in delegating. Here's a rule of thumb: For every three hours of work you want done, you have to log one hour yourself in *managing* the task— even though you can explain it in five minutes. The extra work comes from anticipating contingencies, prioritizing, fielding questions, following up, and so on.

Show your employees what *they* will get out of it. Consult

that assistant about deadlines (let him suggest one; if it's reasonable, he'll feel more bound to it), then, in front of him, mark the dates in your calendar. Explain why he's doing this project, what you are doing, how his work fits in with the overall effort. This is not just to make him feel included, but to give him some sense of priority. Perhaps offer a reward. Encourage—*demand* —that he ask questions. Ask him to tell you in his own words what he is to do.

If he's proven himself to you in the past, then skip this step. Otherwise, explain, in detail, how he should go about getting the job done. And tell him what *not* to do. If he had psychic powers, he'd have a 900 number and wouldn't need this job. Of course your task seems obvious, but rest assured that without instructions, you'll end up with something different from what you wanted.

Divide any long-term projects and give interim deadlines. Mark those dates or times in your calendar for a brief but vital review—has the milestone been met? If not, then why not? When will it be met? Maybe he missed the deadline or did a lousy job. Tell him, yell if you think he'll respond to it, but *be specific*. Precisely where did he screw up? What will he have to do to remedy it?

All of this takes time. You know that. It's just that, God, it's 11 A.M. already, you're overwhelmed with your own work, you have a presentation at 2 P.M. and lunch is already out of the question, and here comes your new assistant and asks what you'd like her to do, and you apologize and say, "Why don't you, um, catch up on the filing, and let's see . . . here, could you make twelve copies of this for me?"

Fifteen minutes later, she's back.

You've got to realize that once you have an employee, delegating is your *first* priority. Sure, at first, you might have to explain a spreadsheet for two hours just to get her to do one hour of work. This is not just an investment, it's vital: One of your charges who simply pushes paper around her desk all day makes *you* look bad. So make time to delegate.

Your First Christmas Party

Most of us adhere to proper decorum during the day-to-day grind. Remember, though, that the Christmas party, the hotel at a company conference, and the parking lot are all extensions of the office. A word to the wise: Think of your first Christmas party as your first day at the beach during the summer. Lots of us let it all hang out, and end up burned as a result. (With a reputation as a promiscuous lush.)

Rx for Procrastination

I send a Mother's Day card, oh, about the first of June. In a best-case scenario, my taxes are filed around 11:50 P.M. on April 15. Christmas shopping tends to get done around December 24—assuming I've planned ahead. I leave my house for the 8:00 train at 7:58 (allocating 20 seconds for the elevator, 48 seconds to retrace my steps and grab my umbrella and then go back to the elevator, 22 seconds to buy a doughnut, and 30 seconds to buy a ticket). Sometimes I miss the train.

Face it: We're all procrastinators, waiting for the "right" time to start that five-mile-a-day running habit or putting off a dentist appointment for months at a time. We feel overwhelmed, we want to do something perfectly, we claim to find "deadline pressure" stimulating. Here are a few tips to stop the procrastinating, both at work and at home.

1. Get started. Sounds simple, but isn't. All beginnings are hard. But what's true in physics is true in life: Once the initial inertia is overcome, a body can stay in motion with less energy.

2. Clear your work area, or your eyes will drift.

3. Television sucks huge quantities of time. You sit there flicking back and forth between MTV and VH-1, while your project looms larger and larger. In the end, you

psych yourself out, sit for hours, and feel worthless. So unplug the TV, even physically turn it facing the wall, and hide the cable box in the linen closet. That way, before you can do any more tube procrastination, you'll have to make so much effort that you'll feel like a *total* loser.

4. Try to give yourself deadlines. This is tough, because you know they're not "real" limits. But if you have a little mental toughness, you can force yourself to do all the dishes before the *90210* rerun comes on.

5. Think of a reward for each self-imposed deadline you meet. It could be an hour to veg and listen to the new R.E.M. disc, it could be a cup of joe from the local Starbucks, it could be a weekend spree in Las Vegas—whatever fits your budget and your achievement.

6. Tap into your moods. Sometimes you're just bursting with energy, bouncing off the walls. Recognize those times and throw yourself into a tough task.

7. If you're stuck on the beginning, try to start in the middle, or at the end. Then work backward.

8. When you've got that big project, don't wait for the ideal, eight-hour block of time. Do small chunks when you can. Break the task down into its smallest components, then knock them off, one at a time.

9. But beware of tip number 8: Don't get stuck making endless "To Do" lists. This is another procrastinating tactic. Just jump in, knock off one job, and cross it off. The pride will give you the energy you need to keep pushing.

10. Sometimes you can plan an event to motivate yourself to finish a chore. For example, since I live alone—in the traditional bachelor-cum-slob mode—I try to have a dinner party every once in a while. That way, my place gets vacuumed at least a few times every year.

11. Find a partner to help. Two people can usually clean two apartments faster than a single person can clean one. You can't get distracted and start reading that *Rolling Stone* you found under the couch when someone else is scrubbing the kitchen floor. To recruit a friend, induce him or her with sex, alcohol, hard cash, or other gifts. According to a Brandeis University study, compact discs are, dollar for dollar, the single most appreciated gift.

Laziness: A True Story

Steve Goldstein is a procrastinator (and my little brother). "When I'm completely overloaded and stressed out, I'll do little tasks and ignore the big stuff," he says. A psychologist would call it fear, fear of something or other—success or failure, perhaps—though I might claim that it's simply genetic. A 1996 graduate of Franklin & Marshall College, Steve says, "It's a matter of what I like. I enjoyed editing our college newspaper, so I stayed on top of everything. I was less enthused about that giant term paper on the economics of the ball-bearing industry due at the end of the semester, so I'd always push it back, back, back, until I was totally paralyzed. There's no easy answer, I guess. At some point, you dive right in. Then when you're done, you think, 'Wow, that wasn't so bad. *Next time* I won't procrastinate.' Of course, you always do."

12. *Everyone* wants to write a novel or make a movie. And *everyone* wants to eat better and work out regularly. You start out running four miles a day for five days. Then you miss a day. You run again for two days; then work piles up and you skip a week. Uh-oh. That worthless feeling washes all over you, right? Just remember that we *all* have trouble with big lifestyle changes, that every good habit is born in little bursts and fits, that start-stop is a common nightmare. Expect setbacks. Just don't let lost battles cost you the war.

13. Don't wait for the "perfect date" to begin—January 1, or Sunday, or whatever. That's setting yourself up for a fall. Once you've decided on a task, dive in without a second thought.

Time-Saving Tips

1. Are you one of millions of Americans who can't function in the morning, even after you've had your Froot Loops? Don't fight it. Just prepare the night before. Around midnight, your eyes may be too tired for reading, your body may even be too spent for sex, but you can always trudge around laying out your clothes, doing any necessary ironing, shoe shining, briefcase packing, and so on.

2. Keep your keys in one place to avoid that frantic, stressful, early-morning treasure hunt.

3. Set your clocks a few minutes ahead—it's amazing how much stress you can preclude by constantly running five minutes ahead of schedule.

4. Don't have meetings without an agenda. You may enjoy meetings when you first start work, since you're doing what you do best—blabbering. But after a year or two, you'll realize that most meetings are big time-wasters, where everyone sounds an opinion but few decisions are made. Good meetings take work. Prepare an agenda, distribute it at least an hour before the meeting, and once the meeting starts, work steadily through the points you've raised. This, no doubt, will require that you cut off debate, vote on a question without a consensus, and move on. In other words, you're going to have to tell people to shut up (in your own soothing way).

5. Personal time is vital to your mental well-being. Don't cheat yourself out of your last gasp of youth (that is, pre-kids) by working around the clock to advance your career.

Yes, I know you want to be CEO and earn 294 kazillion pesos. But you *must* set aside inviolable personal time each day, even if only 20 minutes, for something you enjoy. Aerobics and cleaning don't count. Reading a trashy novel, taking a guitar lesson, playing some two-on-two hoops, relaxing in a bubble bath, lounging and listening to a CD: all are acceptable.

6. Blow up your TV.

7. Don't jump from the middle of one project to the middle of another. Finish something. Anything. One thing. Get it out of the way. Saying "I'm done" is satisfying, which gives you the energy to tackle something new. More important, seeing a single project to the end is efficient: You won't have to constantly review your past work or try to recall where you left off.

8. Don't get bogged down by detail. When you feel yourself descending into a morass of countless hours of work, stop for a few minutes. Do you really need to cross-index your budget in nine different ways?

9. Delegate.

Killing Paperwork (Before It Kills You)

Futurists wax eloquent about the paperless office, where everything is on computer. I don't know—e-mail is definitely a great invention, but for everything else, I like paper. I'd rather read from a hard copy than a screen. I prefer holding a pen, poised to scribble a quick comment on a report, to clicking a mouse. As for vital contracts and other documents, what happens when your hard drive crashes? (Sounds a bit Freudian, I know.) Even more important, if all magazines become electronic, what are you expected to read in the bathroom? Are you supposed to leave an extra laptop lying next to the tub, just so you can retrieve an on-line copy of *Vogue* or *GQ* to pass the time when nature calls?

Paper will never go out of style. So you must learn how to manage it in good health. Paper doesn't just cut people. Paper *drowns* people. How do you stay afloat?

The most important rule is to process each paper as it comes. Don't shuffle the mail around; decide on each piece as it comes, and act on that decision.

- Your *Sports Illustrated* subscription is up? Either renew (and get that free "Making of the Swimsuit Issue" video)—fill in the card, write the check, find a stamp, mail the envelope—or throw it away.
- The season's opera schedule? If you don't think you'll go, don't hang on to the brochure "just in case." Chuck it. If you get the urge to see *Don Giovanni,* you can call for the information—you'd probably never find the mailing anyway.
- A "No openings now" rejection letter from a prospective employer? Make a note on your calendar to try again in two months, then chuck the letter.
- An invitation to a wedding? Make a decision *now.* The fact that the RSVP date is two months away arouses your instinct to wait and see, and then you'll inevitably forget. When you enter the date in your calendar, enter a date the previous week for buying the wedding present.
- A complaint from a customer? Respond immediately and file the letter. Note: This does *not* mean only composing a note on your computer and chucking the customer's letter into a To File bin; print out and mail your response, place the complaint in the proper file and be done with it.
- The information about your Bahamas trip? Staple together the business card, brochure, and price list, leave a message with your girlfriend about discussing plans, and make a note in your calendar to reserve by a certain date.

- *Time* magazine? Try not to read it cover-to-cover. Read what interests you, then chuck the rag. Be selective in your reading; otherwise you'll end up reading so many newspaper and magazine articles, you'll never get around to the cream—books.
- The J. Crew catalog? If you want anything, force yourself to read your piddling bank balance. If you still want something, order it now and toss the catalog. Otherwise, it'll fall into your hands when you're bored or in need of a "purchase high," so you'll end up with three more turtlenecks than you need.
- A personal letter? The best, of course, is to write back directly; otherwise you'll end up "owing" letters. If not, at least address and stamp an envelope, to remind yourself to respond.

MANAGING YOUR DESK

Most of us have two desks in our lives. Your office desk is, of course, the more important. This is where you *live* most of the week. Yet many of you would never leave your bedroom as disgusting as you leave your office desk every night: hopelessly scattered with piles of pages, littered with office supplies, an In box depressingly filled way past capacity.

You probably also have a desk at home (if you don't, you should). The seemingly basic but often violated rule here is to actually *use* it. My folks, for example, own a very nice desk that sits upstairs in the den. It's always five to ten inches deep in paper, however, so Mom stores many of the family's assorted documents on the dining room table. This is kind of a pain when we want to *dine* in the dining room. At that point, we shove all the stacks over to the *kitchen* table—which, by breakfast, must be cleared. . . .

DESK RULES

1. If you're buying a desk, get something wide rather than deep—the latter encourages you to push a stack of particularly boring papers into a far corner, where it might never be seen again.

2. Keep a bulletin board, but only for often-referenced memos or items to be used and disposed of in the next few days. A survey of bulletin boards usually finds them covered with decaying notes circa 1977; don't fall into this trap.

3. Once you finish using files from "dead storage," always return them or they may end up back in your active files.

4. Keep all your brilliant ideas in your calendar in order to prevent a host of Post-it notes from overpopulating your desk.

5. You actually have to set aside time for paperwork. For most people, this time is comparable to the pain of listening to Kathie Lee Gifford while lying on a bed of nails. Yet it must be done, if only for 15 to 30 boring minutes a day.

FILING

Nobody likes to file. But trust me: It's not as bad as spending panicky hours with an IRS goon or a cranky boss breathing down your neck as you shuffle through stacks of paper to find a canceled check or the only copy of an executed contract. Most people have systems, but don't keep up with them. Others keep absolutely every gram of paper that enters their lives, where in their P file you can find all their peppermint patties. (or is that under "Y"). Obsessive filers accumulate paper to the point where finding anything is cumbersome, some documents only one month old are mixed with those from six years ago.

Common categories of files include: banking, bargains, car, computer, contracts, credit, frequent flyer, ideas, insurance, investments, loans, medical, personal, receipts, recipes, reference, résumés, warranties. Alphabetizing and color-coding are common ways to organize.

Neither the individual manila folders, nor those green hanging folders, nor the filing cabinet itself should be stuffed. Again, don't shove papers into an already-full folder. When it bulges so that you can't read its tab, grab a new folder and divide the old one's contents into two.

Use staples instead of paper clips. Clips get stuck on other papers.

You'll constantly have to invent new categories. But don't create so many files that each has exactly one piece of paper in it.

Use ten-by-fifteen-inch envelopes for the various bills and statements that come monthly—from the bank, the phone company, American Express, and so on. That way, once you pay your phone bill, you can simply shove it into the envelope. Keep all canceled checks.

Your most important file will be your income tax returns. *Do not lose them.*

CALENDARS

Use one. Just one. Only one. Not two. One.

Nowadays, people have five or more calendars—the Filofax, the desktop pad, the Apple Newton portable computer, the Far Side wall calendar, the Calendar Creator program on a desktop computer, the Van Gogh pocket calendar, perhaps another wall calendar at home. The problem, naturally, is transferring information.

So buy whichever *single* calendar best suits your needs, whether week-at-a-glance or day-by-day, whether it fits in your pocket or fills a large notebook on your desk.

- Tip: During March, don't carry the empty pages of August; keep them in your desk until they're *needed*.

When scheduling an appointment that will be in an unfamiliar location, write the phone number, address, and directions in your calendar. When you're ten minutes late and running out the door, you don't want to have to poke around for the scrap of paper which has the vital info.

chapter three

Managing Your Paycheck

BUDGETS, BANKING, INVESTING, INSURANCE

Budgets. Banking. Investing. Insurance. Could four more boring words exist in the English language?

Now try these: Jeep Wrangler. Breakfast. Tahiti. Levi's. Much better, right? The point is, you can't have the last four without the first four, so read this chapter about managing your money, and then we'll get on to chapters with good topics, like sex.

Books that cover money management abound; they tend to be several hundred pages long and give advice like "look for a 90-day Commercial Paper rate of 4.6 percent, unless your prospective nonlinear investment horizon calls for SEP/IRA or ConSern loans, as discussed in Appendix III-D-vi." The next few pages provide some basics and a few clever insights. My fundamental suggestion, though, is: You're young, so be aggressive. For example, you can invest in riskier stocks instead of worry-free government bonds. You can skimp on some kinds of insurance. *Take more risks.* If you hit pay dirt, you'll be way ahead of the game; and if not, you'll still have plenty of years before retirement to straighten out your finances. We'll start by examining . . .

Budgeting

The word has an awful ring to it, like *laundry, taxes,* and *Richard Simmons.* But take a lesson from Congress. They're supposed to choose between feeding the homeless or subsidizing college for poor students, between building another MX missile or recruiting 50 more Marines. Those are tough choices. So Congress doesn't make them—which is why we loathe the institution and why we have a multitrillion-dollar national debt.

But in the long run, the choices still have to be made, if only be default. Now, instead of providing either food or education, we provide neither and pay for a third option: interest on the debt.

So learn from our national mistakes. If you don't budget, if you don't make choices, you'll always sacrifice your larger goals—a new car, perhaps—for immediate satisfaction, like Pearl Jam's new double live CD. Yet many of us insist on following a model I call "forced budgeting." My pal Julia, for example, deposits her monthly paycheck, then withdraws $50 every few days from the ATM until the machine flashes "Insufficient Funds." After that, she eats only spaghetti and bagels until her next paycheck.

Here's a simple guide to budgeting, step by glorious step.

STEP 1: WHERE ARE YOU NOW?

Add up your *assets:* bank accounts, stocks and bonds, collectibles (art, jewelry, baseball cards), auto value (what you could sell it for, not what it's worth to you), and so on.

Total your lump-sum *debts:* credit card balances, college

loans, auto loans, outstanding taxes or medical bills, and so on.

Add up your monthly *income:* wages, tips, dividends and interest, and so on.

STEP 2: WHAT ARE YOUR GOALS?

Think about this for a while. Don't worry about dollar amounts (such as "I want to save $5,000 in two years"), but specifics. Some short-term possibilities: an engagement ring, a year of piano lessons, a laptop computer, three ounces of pure Colombian cocaine (hint: piano lessons and often engagement rings are safer). Some long-term aims: a house, grad school, starting a business, retiring at age 50.

You should also plan to set aside an emergency fund, enough to live on for at least three months. You never know when your employer will "downsize"—or when an overbearing or even overheated new boss will show up in your office, and you'll want to leave your job even before securing a new one.

If you can't decide on any goals, try the "10 percent" solution; you take a tenth of your paycheck, and before anything else, deposit that money in a separate savings account. If you can't afford it right away, start with 3 percent on your next paycheck. Then raise it to 6 percent at six months and 10 percent after a year. Once you've put the 10 percent solution in place, you are now free to spend without guilt. You're also free from the common "Will I make it to the first of the month?" stress.

Finally, consider your occupation and its long-term earning potential. A sixth-grade teacher, a real estate agent, and a Wall Street options trader, for example, might all start at $25,000 a year. Yet the teacher will probably never break $50,000; the real estate agent, after a few years of schmoozing at his local St. Mary's and the Moose Club, might be garnering six figures; and the options trader should at some point see her salary rocket past the million mark.

In other words, for those of you on the path to make the big bucks in a few years, a dollar now may be far more valuable than even two dollars down the road. This isn't license to party with abandon, but it does mean that the novice options trader can spend a little more freely, reasonably confident that her income will grow exponentially over the years. The teacher, meanwhile, should start to hoard for retirement right now—with a reasonably certain future of modest income, why wait to start planning?

STEP 3: WHAT ARE YOUR EXPENSES?

Use round numbers, be realistic, and work in pencil. Most of us, on our first attempt, will end up with higher expenses than income and will have to go back and refigure. That's okay. This process takes a few attempts over the course of a couple days. Rare is the guy whose income matches his expense budget on the very first try; that sort of person tends to wear a pocket protector anyway.

Monthly Expenses

Rent: A rule of thumb is to spend about a quarter of your gross income. In cities like New York and San Francisco, you may have to spend a third or even half when you're starting out.

Utilities: Sewage, electricity, cable, water, phone, and so on. Many financial professionals consider this mandatory spending, but this *is* a category you can control. Make long-distance calls after 11 P.M. (and decide beforehand how long you'll stay on); air conditioning consumes huge amounts of energy, so close the blinds on summer days in order to prevent the sunshine from heating your apartment; wear a sweater in the winter and lower the thermostat; fill the dishwater to capacity; and don't stay in the shower long enough to sing a whole album—two songs should be enough.

Insurance: If you have quarterly payments, divide by 3 and put the number here. (In a few pages, we'll look at insurance, and you may decide you have too little . . . or too much.)

Transportation: This includes loan or lease payments, gas, and oil. In New York City, where cars are less common, you still have taxi and subway costs (I average 50 tokens a month, plus the payments on my bulletproof vest).

Dependents: If you support a kid, good luck. You need a serious money book about kids, with details all about saving for college educations. (Zero-coupon bonds, anyone?) I face expenses in *not* starting a family: $15 for condoms and $50 for gifts so my girlfriend doesn't hassle me about marriage.

Medical care: Insurance premiums, prescriptions and over-the-counter drugs, deductibles and co-pays, psychotherapy, and so on.

Home-related expenses: Light bulbs, beer, clothes (including laundry and dry cleaning), toiletries, batteries, food, videotapes, and so on. And beer.

Entertainment: Flicks, compact discs, football games, body-piercing restaurants, nightclubs, skydiving jump fees, and so on.

Debt reduction: Any scheduled monthly payments, plus a portion toward paying off lump-sum debts.

Annual Expenses

These include Christmas and Hanukkah presents, vacations, car tune-ups, dentist appointments, your *Vogue* subscription, a new suit, health club dues, Air Jordans, (anything more than withheld) taxes (and help preparing them), adult education courses, United Way donations, and so on.

STEP 4: CRUNCHING NUMBERS

This is best done by example.

Julia has $5,000 in the bank and two bonds (left over from high-school graduation), which will be worth $1,000 each in two years. She owes $778 on her Visa (there was a "block-buster" sale at Ann Taylor) and $3,300 to the University of North Carolina, which she pays back at $50 per month. After taxes, her assistant publicity manager job earns about $1,900 a month. Her goals: a VCR for $300 and a laptop computer for $900 (short-term); start-up costs of $20,000 for her own public relations firm (long-term).

Monthly Expenses:

Rent	$510
Utilities	120
Transportation	150
Insurance	180
Boyfriend[1]	90
UNC payments	50
Entertainment	350
Home	300
Annual[2]	300
Savings[3]	190
Total	**$2,240**

Uh-oh. She's overbudget by $340 a month!

[1] It sounds like a lot, but he's an actor and doesn't have any money of his own—plus she can't stand his clothes and is always taking him to Banana Republic.

[2] Her annual expenses are around $3,500, including $600 for her health club and $800 for vacations. Divide by 12 (months) to get $300.

[3] She agreed to use the 10 percent rule, so she'll save $190 of her $1900 monthly income.

STEP 5: MAKING ADJUSTMENTS

First, the obvious: Dump the boyfriend. But that could mean higher entertainment costs (no more freebie tickets to plays, much more drinking with the girls), which means late-night taxis (more transportation costs). Also, without him her electric bill would be higher (she'll need more heat).

Instead, she weans herself from the Columbia Records mail-order club, cold turkey. That was $50 a month. She figures the grunge look is actually cool and saves $40 on Banana Republic for the boyfriend. She packs her lunch—$20 salvaged—and limits her trips to restaurants and bars to twice a week—another $60. Since she doesn't use the health club anyway, she quits. That's $600 a year, or $50 a month.

Still not enough—$120 to go. She steals a can of Mace from her friend, and then cuts out Saturday night taxis—$40. She reads the section in this book on insurance and cuts out $30. Despite my protestations, she cuts her monthly contribution to her savings account from $190 to $140, yielding an extra $50 per month. So, in the end, she's cut that stubborn $120—$40 plus $30 plus $50—so now her budget balances.

STEP 6: WHAT SHOULD JULIA (AND YOU) DO WITH THE $140 A MONTH THAT SHE'S NOW SAVING?

First, get rid of credit card debt. The interest rates are usually outrageous. It'll take about six months to retire that $778; but if she doesn't deal with it, her debt will rise to $900 within a year.

Next, she should set aside three months' salary—$5,700—as an emergency fund. Already she's got $5000 in the bank, so in five months at $140 each, she'll be up to speed.

That leaves one month left in the year unspoken for—just $140, not even enough for the VCR. Well, not quite. She's got $5,000 in savings. Should she be earning interest on that? Damn straight. We'll cover that in just a couple of paragraphs, but for this example, if Julia keeps $3,000 in the bank at 3 percent interest, and $2,000 in a mutual fund at 7 percent, that's another $230 in added income at the end of the year. Add it to that $140 in uncommitted savings, and she can get the VCR. Plus she's in great shape for next year. (Unless Ann Taylor has another blockbuster sale.)

In the end, a budget is like a diet. You need to honestly assess where you are, set specific goals, keep written track of your purchases and your meals (and your snacks). Just as you break a diet sometimes, you'll break your budget, too. Don't be discouraged and quit when that happens. It's natural.

At our age, it's hard to give a damn about budgets. But remember, you're setting financial habits that will last a lifetime. Again, think nutrition: Everyone knows a few skinny people with high metabolism, who eat like pigs and never gain a pound. In the end, those skinny people turn into fat slobs, because when their metabolisms slow down, their bad habits of burgers and fries are pretty hard to shake.

Here are a couple of final tips. First, don't carry a lot of cash. You withdraw $100 on Monday—it's supposed to last until Friday—but by Wednesday at lunchtime, you're down to $8.73. What happened? The new Juliana Hatfield CD, a silk scarf for half price, pay-up time for the neighbor's walkathon, and a Tuesday night that was supposed to be a quick drink with Tom but turned into four margaritas and a large order of nachos. Take only a couple of days' cash with you; leave the rest at home.

Second, leave your ATM card at home. *At home?* What if you absolutely *need* to buy that antique photo frame, and it's only on sale *today,* and if you don't get it now someone else who wasn't even there first will capitalize on your loss? If you don't have your ATM card, you can't make even the most perfect impulse buy—which is exactly the point.

Banking

Since the first time Mom gave you an allowance, you were probably encouraged to do that most un-American of activities: save money. The few coins left over after the requisite Barbie apparel and Chewbacca Action Figure purchases went into the piggy bank. Then, as you grew older, babysitting, adoring grandparents, lawn mowing, newspaper delivery, bat mitzvahs, and that lunch money extortion racket generated enough money to require . . . a savings account. It paid 5 1/2 percent interest, by law.

Things are less simple these days. Banks have been deregulated and offer different (and constantly changing) rates of interest and charge various fees. True, most of us aren't rich—yet. So why waste time figuring out what to do with your lousy $400 a week when you could be watching *Cheers* reruns?

Because with the money you're wasting, you may be able to afford a new television *and* cable—and then you can watch *Beavis and Butt-Head*.

A bank essentially makes money like this: They pay you for deposits at, say, 3 percent interest, then lend your money to borrowers, at, say, 12 percent. The bigger the deposits, the better—more money to lend, more profit. That's why most banks aren't particularly interested in the piddly $2,675.43 you have; they have better things to do than waste time processing your little $25 checks, mail you all those statements, and so on.

So some banks charge fees for checking accounts, and that's the most important thing for the small-timer to avoid in choosing (or changing) a bank. Make sure you get free checking, often called a NOW account. For a minimum balance—which varies, usually from $3,000 down to zip—you avoid fees for ATM transactions (even from machines that aren't owned by your bank), for checks paid, or for the dreaded monthly service charge.

If you don't maintain that minimum, then a typical month in which you write eight checks, for example, and use the ATM machine a half-dozen times, would cost you a service charge of $20 to $25. That's upwards of $250 a year for First National Pinstripe to hold *your* money! You'd almost be better off keeping it under your mattress.

ATM costs are changing quickly. More banks are moving in the direction of waiving fees for all ATM transactions. Why? They want to encourage you to stay away from the tellers—humans cost more than computers. In fact, one Chicago bank announced in 1995 that it would start *charging* customers *extra* to do banking with tellers. That might be the wave of the future, or, conversely, banks might begin to discount transactions done over the computer, by telephone, or by ATM. If you're not looking for a friendly face at the bank anyway, the coming years could bring your significant banking savings if you shop around.

Also, it's worth a few phone calls to find a bank that will pay you interest on your fledgling checking account. If you earn just 3 percent a year, and keep a $3,000 minimum in the bank, that's $90 a year in easy money.

Money management books dwell on other, more complicated issues, like how often your interest is *compounded,* or multiplied. Usually banks calculate interest on a daily or monthly basis. Compounding is totally irrelevant to the small-timer. The difference between your $3,000 being compounded daily versus monthly is a whopping three bucks a year. You're much more interested in customer service, like how long you'll wait in line. Some banks offer "guarantees," like $5 cash for any customer who has to wait more than seven minutes. Does yours?

It's worth mentioning that "FDIC" means that Uncle Sam guarantees your deposits; the fear is not Jesse James types, but that your bank could fold, which does happen occasionally when greedy financiers make a lot of risky loans. The FDIC guarantees deposits up to $100,000. If you have more than that, you probably don't have to read this book, but just in case you've just won the Lotto, spread your winnings around in different banks—not different *branches,* but different *banks.*

Credit unions are often better than banks. They're like banks in virtually every respect, except they have members— their customers—instead of outside, profit-hungry shareholders. This, in turn, means lower rates for loans and higher rates for deposits. The FDIC does *not* cover credit unions, so make sure they're insured by the National Credit Unions of America by calling the Massachusetts Credit Union Association at 800-842-1242. You can also use that number to find a credit union near you that you may be eligible to join. Not everyone can join: You have to be a member of an employee union or some sort of association. The largest credit unions tend to be those of government employees.

CONSOLIDATING SCHOOL LOANS

When Dennis Gantry graduated from Penn State in 1994, he owed $17,000 for his education. By autumn, he'd lined up a job in Chicago as a social worker, which paid $24,000 a year. He had a girlfriend. Penn State had yet another good football team. Dennis was happy.

Then he started getting bills for his student loans; it was payback time. Fifty bucks here, $80 there, $30 from yet another lender. They added up to just under $300 a month. After taxes, he was earning $1,300 a month, and the student loan payments were consuming a huge chunk of that. What with rent, car expenses, and just some basic grub, Dennis was hurting for cash. He encouraged his girlfriend to take a second job, but to no avail.

So he consolidated his various loans through Sallie Mae (the Student Loan Marketing Association). This program has three advantages: a lower rate, a longer payment schedule, and less paperwork. He's now paying around $150 a month with a single check—obviously the trade-off is that it will take longer to pay off, so he'll ultimately pay thousands more in interest over the years. But for now, he's got a bit of breathing room. In other words, he has some cash flow. Consolidating loans isn't magic, but it can be useful for recent grads—so proceed with caution.

THE BALANCING ACT

Do you balance your checkbook? Should you? My girlfriend uses her patented Hope and Pray™ method; she deposits her paycheck, pays her rent and a few bills, and hopes there's enough in her account that the checks don't bounce.

That's a bad idea, for two reasons. First, the bank makes mistakes. They may lose or mis-enter one of your deposits, overcharge you for fees, and so on. Second, some merchants aren't timely about cashing your checks. If you just look at the balance on your bank statement, you don't know how much is *really* there, because you may have a few outstanding checks.

Balancing isn't very complicated. But it is a pain in the neck. Ideally, according to the experts, you should balance the checkbook every time you make any transaction. Realistically, this is slightly more feasible than dunking a basketball with Shaquille in your face.

It's more likely that you'll balance once a month, first calculating your balance on your own, then comparing against the bank statement. How? First, look at your checkbook and subtract any checks written. Second, gather your ATM receipts and subtract those withdrawals, too. Then subtract any monthly wire transfers or automatic withdrawals (perhaps your health club). Next, add up your (usually pink) deposit receipts and *add* them to your balance.

When the bank statement arrives in the mail, you have one more step: deducting any transaction and service fees. Then compare your version of the balance to the bank's version. This is called *reconciling*. When the two numbers differ, it's often just a check or two that you've written but hasn't yet been processed. Or you lost an ATM receipt. Sometimes, though, you'll catch a mistake. It tends not to be in your favor. Double-check your math, and if you still can't get the numbers to match, go to see a customer service agent. They tend to be about as friendly as Sam Donaldson, but you can push them around by asking for their "superior." Then they'll play ball.

One Person's Tale of Electronic Banking Woe

Marla is a marketing assistant for a Broadway theater producer. "I tried to do the bank-by-phone thing and to use banking software," she says of a popular checkbook computer software program (you type in all the information; the computer prints the checks and keeps track of your bank balance). "It worked out about as well as when I was fifteen and tried to dye my hair red. Even though I used it successfully at work, where we have dozens of checks to write every day, it was a pain to boot up my home computer just to print out a single lousy check. And sometimes you just want to bring a blank check in your purse—which sort of defeats the purpose of the program. Plus, my checks were sometimes getting stuck in the printer, or they'd be misaligned, so I was voiding check after check. As for the on-line checking, I couldn't get help from customer service; my modem would sometimes disconnect. In the end, I decided that waiting five minutes in line at the bank maybe wasn't such a big deal, so I went back to the old-fashioned way. I write checks by hand."

The real problem with check-balancing is ATM machines. It's easier for purse-toting women to carry their checkbooks around with them, and thus to immediately deduct their ATM withdrawals from their balance. Men need to hang onto the receipts, which might easily number five or ten over a month. Lose a single one and your balance is off.

For the computer-literate, there are various software packages to keep your financial life in order. The most popular, Quicken, takes care of the terrifying math, prints checks, and the like. Wealthier types will find that Quicken shows you alternatives whenever you enter an investment or pay taxes. If the software is combined with a modem, credit card charges can be entered automatically, bills can be paid automatically, and stock prices can even be imported from Prodigy. If you do decide to get one of these programs, *back up your data*. Trust me: When your computer lights up with a "Hard Drive Controller Failure" message and you've lost years' worth of checkbooks, you're not going to be happy (and neither is the IRS).

OVERDRAFTS

Let's face it: Some of you readers are financial slobs. You may have read this far, but know deep down that you aren't going to be balancing checkbooks, that you're going to live from one paycheck to the next. Okay. Then think about *overdraft protection*. It means that if you bounce a check, the bank will cover it for you, so it won't *really* bounce. Overdraft protection is automatic credit. Since a single bounced check can cost you a bundle in penalties—the bank will hit you for $20, and Kmart might hit you for another $30—the overdraft protection is great insurance.

Usually, there's no annual fee for this service. The bank makes money by charging you huge rates for any unpaid overdraft balances. So if you bounce a rent check for $500, the bank will charge you interest on that sum, from the day you bounce. In other words, overdraft protection is a high-rate loan that automatically kicks in when you need it.

In short, if you live your life check-to-check, get overdraft protection as "insurance" so you'll never actually bounce a check, but *never* keep an overdraft balance—you'll get fleeced.

CREDIT CARDS

And finally, a few words on credit cards. Did you ever open your mailbox and find one of these?

Dear College Student or Recent Grad:
Enclosed is your preapproved Visa card! Yes, we know you have no cash—in fact, you're probably up to your ears in college loans. Who cares? We don't. Head out to Circuit

City or The Gap, buy yourself that CD player and a new fall wardrobe—it's on us! That way, you'll accumulate a few thousand bucks in debt, pay us outrageous interest rates [sometimes double a regular loan rate!] for many months, and perhaps go crawling to Mom and Dad, who will send us a big check and cut up your card.

But if that happens, don't worry, because we'll send you another preapproved card! So buy now and worry later—it's the American way.

You probably don't need a lecture, but remember: A credit card is supposed to be a convenience. It is not a source of income. And you really should pay off your balance every month. We all know the score—the card shows up in your mailbox; you didn't even ask for it. Hey, you're just delighted to get any mail at all. Then it takes just one 800 call to activate it. So easy. The banks basically give us the rope; many of us go ahead and hang ourselves (then get Ma and Pa to bail us out).

Picking a Credit Card

Don't get me wrong. You need credit cards for hotel rooms, rental cars, roses for Mother's Day, airline tickets, and a host of other products; you also need them so you don't have to risk carrying around a lot of cash.

But the banks make plenty of dough on credit cards from the merchant side. They take money off the top from the vendor, usually around 2 percent of the sale (that's one reason why stores prefer cash). So don't let First National Pinstripe get even richer by taking an annual fee from you; there are plenty of free Visas and MasterCards. (Look in any issue of *Money* magazine for a list, or, even better, get a card from AT&T or one of the phone companies, from an airline, from GM or Ford, or from General Electric—where you'll get miles or long-distance minutes or credits for every dollar you charge.)

Nobody begins by planning to max out his or her cards. Some clothes, some gas, a computer repair, an initiation fee at the gym—soon it adds up. If you're stuck at the limit, you might be unpleasantly surprised to find that on many cards, the bank can raise your interest rate.

Don't use your credit card for a cash advance; stick with your ATM card. Don't pay late fees; it's $10 or $20 a pop just because you procrastinated. Don't pay fees for exceeding your limit; if you need to make a huge charge, you often can get your limit raised with a single phone call to the toll-free number on the back of your card.

And, to reiterate, *do not* carry a balance from month to month. It's simply a loan at a terrible rate. If you insist on doing it, find a card with a low APR (annual percentage rate) and make sure that the bank excludes new purchases when it calculates your balance for its finance charge. That is, if you owe $500 from six weeks ago, and you charged another $250 a week ago, don't let them calculate their fee on the basis of $750.

Another trick: You usually have a grace period—25 days is standard—from the date the bill is mailed until your check is due. So make any big purchases immediately after the bill gets sent out. If they mail your bills on the fifteenth, for example, charge your refrigerator on the sixteenth. That way you'll have a full month plus the 25 days to pay your tab.

American Express is a little bit different. It's a debit card, which means you have to pay your balance in full each month. They also employ a macho marketing tactic, offering gold and even platinum cards for "a select few." What does a platinum card provide for its $300 annual fee? Despite all their hyped services, the only real benefit is "status." So don't waste your money on "premium" cards.

In-Store Cards

You've seen those "No money down, no interest for one full year!" ads, favorite of the computer and appliance industry. Usually, the deal goes something like this: Crazy Charlie's Appliance Dome offers you an in-store preferred charge card, with no interest for, say, six months. You are already carrying a Visa balance, and you're expecting a big birthday present in three months, so you go ahead and buy that PowerBook you've been eyeing, at $1,450.

You even check the fine print for the APR (annual percentage rate), and find that it's 18 percent—high, but not outrageous, and you're planning to pay off the card before your six months are up anyway, so the interest is irrelevant.

Six months pass. You've been enjoying the PowerBook, writing your Great American Novel at the local Starbucks, and you've paid off $750 already. Things are a bit tight right now, but you're getting a sales bonus in three weeks, so you'll wait until then to pay the $700 remaining, even if Crazy Charlie will charge you $10.50 for one month of financing (since your six months are up).

Surprise! When you get the bill, chances are the finance charge will be around $75! Why? Most in-store cards make you pay the interest *retroactively.* The "free" six months apply only if your balance is paid in full. Otherwise, you'll be charged for back interest at the 18 percent APR on whatever balance you have remaining at the end of the "free" period.

Credit Ratings

Every time you make a late payment on your credit card, you hurt your credit rating. Three major bureaus keep records on virtually everyone who has ever borrowed money; they monitor how fast you repay student loans, auto loans, credit card debts, and the like.

Credit ratings are sometimes called The Three Cs—character, capacity, and capital. *Character* sizes up how responsible you've been, not just if and when you've paid, but how much you charged in the first place. If you're grossing $30,000 a year and have Visa bills totaling $10,000, it doesn't speak well of you, even if you pay in full.

Capacity is income, including dividends, alimony, trust funds, and the like. *Capital* is assets like stocks, cars, your baseball card collection—anything that the bank could seize if you default on your loan.

These ratings translate into big bucks when you want to buy a house. For example, suppose you're seeking a $100,000 loan for that dream pad. Maybe the bank usually charges 12 percent, but since you've made late payments on your college loans six times, they check your credit rating and figure you're a little more risky. So they charge you 13 percent. That means you'll pay an extra grand a year over the course of your 30-year mortgage!

Even if you do falter, don't ever believe companies advertising "credit repair." It sounds tempting, but is actually a whole industry of various scams and deceits, offering various financial services (like "debt counseling") and promising to change your credit rating. Don't do it. They *cannot* improve your rating, except by using a process called "file segregation," which is actually tampering and definitely illegal.

The three credit bureaus are Experian (formerly TRW) in Orange, CA (800-422-4879); Equifax in Atlanta, GA (800-685-1111); and Trans Union in Chicago (312-258-1717). By law, they must provide you with a copy of your credit report if you request it.

Investing

All of the hundreds of books, magazines, newsletters, and television programs devoted to investing create an impression: that whether you're into stocks, bonds, real estate, or gold, investing is terribly complicated. It's not.

Rule 1: The higher the reward, the riskier the investment.

This is an axiom of "There's no such thing as a free lunch." A savings account at First National Pinstripe is just about the safest investment around, and in return, you earn a measly 2 percent or so. On the other hand, SuperCyberStuff, a young, volatile stock, might double in value over the course of a year. Or it might go bust.

Being young, you might well be comfortable with risk, and might therefore give your money a chance to rocket in value. Or you might want to play it safe. As a famous economist once said, you essentially have a choice between eating well and sleeping well.

Low risk   Certificates of deposit, Treasury bills, bank accounts, money market accounts, most bonds.
Medium risk Certain mutual funds, blue-chip stocks (in Coca-Cola, for example).
High risk   Stocks in new or small companies, especially high-tech businesses; commodities like gold or oil.

Rule 2: Nobody knows anything.

The screenwriter William Goldman said this about Hollywood, but it applies here too. This, I realize, is tough to swallow. What about the editors of *The Wall Street Journal,* or the CEO of Merrill Lynch, or the chairman of the SEC? Surely these guys know something.

They do. But the problem is, a lot of other people know the same things. "Efficient market theory," widely accepted among economists and detested among brokers, says that because the information flow is nearly perfect, no one can get a leg up on the next person. This theory holds that by throwing darts at the newspaper's stock listing page, you can pick just as well as your broker. Efficient market theory dictates there's no such thing as a "hot tip."

Let's say, for example, that your uncle, a court clerk in Alaska, calls you excitedly one morning to tell you that he had read a draft opinion, and the judge was planning to hit Exxon with a $5 billion fine for their Valdez shenanigans. You own 100 shares. "Sell!" he hisses. You do.

In real life, when the judge announced the fine, guess what happened? Wrong. Exxon stock actually went *up,* because "the market" had already estimated the possible loss, and $5 billion fell short of what they thought the court *might* do. In other words, Wall Street thought the fine might be $10 billion, so they were *relieved* at $5 billion. So given the oil giant could afford that whopping fine, and that the cloud of doubt over the company had been removed, brokers moved to *buy* Exxon stock.

Again, efficient market theory tells you not to worry about hot tips. (The exception is insider trading, which is, of course, illegal.) There may not be any surefire get-rich-quick investment winners, but there are some guidelines to avoiding likely losers.

STOCKS

The New York Stock Exchange, NASDAQ, and the American Stock Exchange are not the volatile, murky places you think they are. Stock is part ownership of a company. You make money in two ways. First, if the stock price rises, you can sell it at a profit; second, every year, if the company is profitable, it may pay "dividends," or your share of that profit.

Even though you're part owner, only investors holding huge amounts of shares, often in the millions, tend to have any say or influence on the company's management.

The price is based on the outlook for the company; if advance word on IBM's new PC-15 is hot, more people buy the stock, and the higher the price goes.

There are many stock strategies; most are contradictory. If Lockhead is trading at its all-time low, some would argue that now is the time to buy: get the bargain while it's out of favor. Others would urge you to follow the direction of the market: many people have soured on Lockhead, so they may know something that you don't.

On one hand, many money managers encourage you to do your own research: Is the company offering new products soon? Is it deeply in debt? What is the management record? Is there labor trouble in the horizon? Is the company for sale?

The "gurus" tell you to look at the balance sheet. They tell you to analyze the current ratio of debt (what the company owes) to equity (how much the company is worth), where a debt-to-equity ratio of more than 3 to 1 is "too high." They tell you to examine P/E ratios (that's price versus earnings-per-share: a P/E below 10 means the market doesn't expect much growth in the stock; above 15 means everyone is hot on that company). The "gurus" invoke price-action theories, trading volume, ROEs, dividend payout ratios, and other mind-numbing mumbo jumbo.

The problem with all this research is, other analysts have already done it! They've done their homework, they update it night and day, and their opinions are reflected in the stock's current price.

The only way you can get an edge is if you think you know something the analyst doesn't. Perhaps you can use your personal observation; if you live across the street from a new fast-food joint called Au Bon Pain, and business is booming, perhaps you'd want to buy.

Peter Lynch, perhaps the most successful stock picker of all time, is a folksy guy. He retired after thirteen years with the Fidelity Magellan fund, the world's largest mutual fund. His motto: "Never invest in any idea that you can't illustrate with a crayon." Lynch tells of going to the local Toys R Us and looking for a crowd of kids. If they're clamoring for Mattel's new Super Mario Kick-Boxing Knife-Wielding Iraqi Secret Service, he might buy Mattel. If Hasbro's Billy the Mauve Giraffe seems to be the next Barney, Lynch might buy their stock.

Here are a few basics.

1. **Buy for the long term.** First of all, each time you buy or sell, your broker takes a commission, so you want to minimize those fees. More important, you're trying to find healthy companies, so it makes sense to stick with them, rather than trying to win short-term gains, then resuming your research to find yet another healthy company.

2. **Buy it all at once.** This directly contradicts many money managers, who suggest buying a little bit of the same stock every month, or "dollar cost averaging." DCA does reduce risk (which you're less worried about than your parents or grandparents are) but costs more in broker's fees, which you want to keep down.

3. **Have target selling prices.** Anywhere from 25 to 50 percent appreciation is a fair goal. If you buy at $10 per share, pick your sale price right away—maybe $14 per share—and *write it down.* There is a very strong psychological tendency for individual investors to hold a stock too long. If you decide in advance at what price you'll sell, you won't have any sleepless nights.

    The stock market behaves much like a casino. Caesar's gets rich more from psychology than odds: you play for an hour, you're up $200. But you play on, because you didn't decide *in advance* when you'd quit. And it seems like easy money. An hour (and three "free" drinks) later, you're still ahead, but only by $50. Since you tasted the $200, you desperately want to get back there—*then,* you tell yourself, you'll quit. Unfortunately, in another hour, you're down $300, which is all you brought, so you *can't* play anymore.

4. **Look for younger businesses.** Younger businesses grow and provide the chance for large price appreciation. "Income stocks," like utilities and banks, are safer: they don't vary much in price but tend to pay high, consistent dividends.

5. **Use discount brokers.** A "full-service" broker, like Smith Barney Shearson, provides walk-in branches, IRAs, Keoghs, analyst opinions, asset management, and other services. But discount brokers like Charles Schwab offer all of that—except analyst opinions—yet they take commissions of 20 to 60 percent less. And perhaps they provide a little less hand-holding.

Spencer, 29, tells this story. "Once upon a time, I had $6,000 to invest. For six months, I kept it in a CD [certificate of deposit]. When it was due for renewal, I had earned just $150 in interest, and was looking for more. But I had only a two-week window to pull out my money; otherwise the bank was going to reinvest my money in the CD automatically. I decided to play the stock market.

"My friend Mark, a Wall Street analyst, had recommended Urban Outfitters, which was then selling for about $20 a share. Mark's logic was this: 'A bunch of MBA grads from the Wharton School started that company several years ago. Now they just sold all their shares. When executives sell or buy in their own company, they must report it to the stock market authorities. So when Wall Street sees the company's own insiders are selling, they figure something must be wrong, so *they* sell, too, and the price goes down. I'm figuring, though, that these Wharton guys are just looking for a new challenge. So I think the price should not have dropped to $20, I think its true value is more like $30, so buy now.'

"I did," Spencer continues. "Grabbed 150 shares. Then I watched it, every day, for months. It soon rose to $25 per share, where it stayed for about four months. Then I had to sell it because I was out of cash—turning a $750 profit. Not bad, though it did go even higher a few months later. Still, I was happy to have made money."

Spencer adds, "I guess I'd be pulling a fast one if I didn't tell you about my other purchase: Flagstar, the company that owns Denny's, Hardee's, and some other restaurant chains. I read in a financial magazine that some smart guy thought it would go to $17 a share; it was selling at $6. Wow, what a deal! Plus, we're a nation of gluttons, so I figured combining Denny's and Hardee's couldn't be a bad move. I bought 400 shares and waited, figuring I'd sell when it went to $15—I wasn't going to be greedy. Flagstar promptly fell to $3 a share. Now I don't count on magazines anymore."

Some brokers give further discounts for *telebrokering*: executing your stock trade through a computer instead of a human being. Schwab, for example, offers an additional 10 percent discount.

6. **Don't buy on margin.** Buying "on margin" is the equivalent of using a Nordstrom's charge card; you might end up on the line for more than you bargained for. Buying on margin is simply making a down payment on a stock and borrowing the balance from the broker. The interest is too high to make sense for anything but the quick kill. So reread tip number 1.

7. **Look for DRIPs (dividend reinvestment plans).** That means your dividends will be automatically reinvested into the stock, usually without a broker's fee. Some stocks offer a sweetened DRIP, where they'll actually discount your reinvestment at up to 5 percent. So if you earn $100 in dividends, they'll reinvest $105. To find these sweetened DRIPs, try the DRIP investor newsletter, *Dow Theory Forecasts*, 7412 Calumet Ave., Hammond, IN 46324, 219-931-6480 or 800-711-7503. The newsletter also lists stocks that you can buy directly from the corporation, like Texaco, without any broker's fees.

MUTUAL FUNDS

A mutual fund essentially picks the stocks for you. You buy shares of the fund; its experts, in turn, buy a portfolio of stocks. One advantage: instant diversification. Another plus: the mutual fund often holds so much stock that it affects corporate decisions—it might, for example, be able to prevent a company president from paying himself $100 million a year. Finally, mutual funds offer low transaction costs; because they buy so much at once, their commissions are as much as ten times lower than *yours* from an individual broker.

Look for a *no-load* fund. You bypass the broker's 4 percent or so commission and buy from the fund directly, usually through an 800 number. You don't get professional advice, but you can pick funds on your own from recommendations in magazines such as *Barron's, Money, Smart Money, Worth,* and so on. (In spite of Spencer's story, magazines are often a terrific source of information.) In 1995, a new magazine called *P.O.V.* was launched—its aim is to be the first financial magazines for twentysomethings. If *P.O.V.* survives (many start-up publications don't), then you'll have a source that explains investing in plain English—no small feat.

Whether you buy a load or no-load fund, there's always a *management fee,* usually around 1 percent annually (don't pay more than 1.25 percent). *Back-end loads* are usually on a sliding scale, where if you want to sell your fund soon after you buy it, the brokerage firm can recoup some of the management fees it expected. You might pay a 4 percent back load if you sell after one year, 3 percent after the second year, and so on, down to nothing if you hold the fund for more than four years.

Avoid *dividend reinvestment loads,* which mean the fund takes a commission for doing nothing but reinvesting any income you've generated. Also avoid *12b-1 fees* (charges for advertising and the like).

The major fund companies are Fidelity, Vanguard, T. Rowe Price, and Dreyfus. To pick a fund—whether you're acting on hearsay, on professional advice, on magazine tips, or whatever—you need to think about the following:

1. **Objective.** There are three basic categories—in order of volatility, they are Income, Growth, and Aggressive Growth. The more volatile the category, the more money you can make—or lose. Most fund companies suggest holding Aggressive Growth funds with a long-term horizon—ten years. They'll tell you that if an Aggressive fund doesn't perform well over the first few years, you have to be willing to wait it out and things will even out over the long term.

2. **Methods.** Which types of stocks will or won't the fund buy? If you think that biotech miracle drugs will soon start flooding the market, you might pick a fund that specializes in high tech. If you think that Hong Kong companies will explode in value even after the Chinese take over in 1997, then go for an appropriate Far East fund. If you don't have a clue, there are basic funds—some buy only major American companies (like AT&T), some focus on small companies, and so on.

3. **Fees.** Again, you want to know how much of your investment the mutual fund gets to keep.

4. **Minimums.** You can buy into many funds for as little as $500 to $1,000. Others require $10,000 or more.

All of this information is contained in each fund's *prospectus* (its sales literature), along with any tax benefits and the fund's performance over the past ten years. Remember: Past performance is certainly no guarantee of future performance.

Mutual Affection

Kate, 25, says, "I basically take recommendations from my dad's broker, or if I hear about something interesting I'll ask her. The broker will ask, 'How aggressive do you want to be? How much would you be willing to lose? Would you be comfortable losing 25 percent?' I stick with mutual funds. So far, things have worked out well. The only one that didn't was this Europe fund [investments in European companies], which I got myself out of. I know you're supposed to wait it out, but I got impatient, and took a loss of maybe 10 percent. I keep following the Europe fund, even if I don't own it anymore—now I'm rooting for it to perform poorly. I put that money into a Latin American fund [run by Scudder, which is one of the larger mutual fund concerns], which is supposed to be very high-risk."

MUTUAL FUND TRICKS

One thing to look out for: Of the three types of funds (different companies have more classifications)—Income, Growth, and Aggressive Growth—many funds have an incentive to misclassify themselves. Why? Look at any fund advertising—in *The Wall Street Journal, Business Week,* and *The New York Times,* and *Money* magazine—and you'll find funds that compare themselves to other funds in the same "category." The Warburg, Pincus "Growth and Income" fund, for example, might show an impressive 17 percent return over the last three years, beating similar "Growth" funds from Fidelity, T. Rowe Price, Vanguard, and other industry giants. Sounds good, right?

Well, take a closer look at Warburg's actual stock holdings and you'd find big chunks of Micron Technology and National Semiconductor—which, at least in 1994, were very high-risk. In other words, the Warburg fund was very aggressive. But by calling this fund "Growth" instead of "Aggressive Growth," they rank at the very top of the "Growth" category, instead of in the middle of "Aggressive Growth." It's like a fifteen-year-old swimmer who competes in the under-thirteens—of course she has a much better chance to "win." The aggressive "wolf" fund wears a low-risk "sheep's" clothing. As *Worth* magazine explains, "The best way to win a contest for largest tomato is to paint a cantaloupe red."

For you, the problem is that you're buying a riskier fund than you wanted. One study found that more than half the funds are misclassified in their advertising, and that 11 percent are at least *two* categories of risk away from their proper place. In other words, 11 percent of mutual funds are calling themselves vanilla frozen yogurt, when they're not yogurt at all, or even vanilla ice cream—they're hot-fudge sundaes.

If you really want to know how risky the fund is, go beyond how the fund classifies itself and look at its actual gains for each of the past five years. If the numbers are consistent—5 percent gain one year, 8 percent the next, then 6 percent, say—

then it's obviously more conservative than a fund that goes up 38 percent one year and down 14 percent the next.

If this sounds way too complicated, try this: Buy a fund that's one category less aggressive than you think you want. Also, you're partially protected since the financial services that tally up (that is, keep score of) the mutual fund rankings—Lipper and Morningstar being the two main ones—constantly reclassify funds that are far out of place.

Another mutual fund tip: Past performance proves nothing. It's like cards—just because your last hand was a straight flush doesn't mean that this hand will be anything more than a pair of twos. The funds that perform well in 1995 buy *lots* of ads during 1996, while the ones that lose money lie low—until they have a winning year. So not only do last year's winners have an even chance of being this year's losers, but they face a flood of investors who react to those ads. So when Moe Green's Casino Fund rakes in a 35 percent return and advertises it, $50 million from eager new investors might pour into the fund. That means Moe has to find somewhere to spend the $50 million. Spending that kind of cash may not sound like a problem to you, but the fact is Moe may only know of $10 million in good opportunities. The remaining $40 million might well be mismanaged, and rushed into companies that he's not so sure of.

Since we are in the socially and environmentally responsible phase of our lives, be aware that some funds search only for profitable *ethical* companies. A few of the more prominent types of these funds are Calvert Ariel Appreciation (800-368-2748), Dreyfus Third World (800-645-6561), Pax World (800-767-1729), and Progressive Environ (800-826-8154).

A cautionary note: Wall Street has fads, not unlike music. They keep coming up with new, high-risk ways of borrowing and lending money. The 1980s fever was for junk bonds; for the 1990s, "derivatives" are in vogue. You should probably steer clear of any fund involved with the fads; it's sort of an "Emperor's New Clothes" deal. The fad, at some point, always collapses. Just like you wouldn't want to be a silk screener holding

5,000 Devo T-shirts in 1995, don't buy funds that are overly risky.

Indulge me for only a quick, preachy paragraph or two. The sad paradox of money is that the more you make, the more you're trapped. You get a raise and immediately look to upgrade your everyday belongings: the shared functional $500-a-month, one-bedroom apartment in a decent part of town becomes the solo, $1,200-a-month, fourteen-foot-ceilinged pad with a view; the seven-year-old Ford Escort becomes a two-year-old Mustang convertible; the Gap card becomes a Saks card.

Don't fall into this trap. Probably 95 percent of Americans do fall into this funk, so it won't be easy for you to avoid. Upward mobility shouldn't mean simply accumulating fatter car payments or larger mortgages just because you can afford them. Once a few weeks go by and you're used to the beautiful view, you'll stop appreciating it. You just will. That's human nature. Not to sound New Age, but as your income grows, you should try to grow yourself, not your collection o' stuff. Indulge your dreams about what you could *become*, not what you could *own*. Take photography or guitar lessons. Go on a hiking trip through the Peruvian rain forests. Save a couple grand and shoot the movie script currently serving a life sentence in your desk drawer.

Whew, thanks. Okay, no more soapbox.

Insurance

What's the most unappealing, dull task you can imagine? Cleaning restrooms, perhaps. Or washing dishes. Loading bolts into boxes, one handful after another, day after gray day.

Now for $10,000, would you scour the Army's filthiest latrines for a week? Of course.

Think of shopping for insurance the same way. It's confusing, loaded with jargon and complex presentation. Yet over the course of your life, you'll likely spend more on insurance than on anything else, besides your house. A certain brother of mine, who shall remain nameless (but rhymes with *even*), spends untold days searching for the perfect car—test-driving and negotiating and pouring over *Motor Trend* and *Consumer Reports*. This same brother bought life insurance in about an hour and a half, with the kind of pensive self-reflection usually associated with Homer Simpson.

By taking time to compare prices and policies, you'll save thousands. Better yet, you'll get the right coverage: not too much, not too little, not duplicated, from companies that will last longer than you do. And, at least while you're young, the right coverage is probably very little coverage.

If you're lucky, and no tragedy ever befalls you, you'll feel like you're wasting your money. Since insurance companies essentially pool risk and spread it around, everyone who escapes sickness, fire, theft, and other calamities subsidizes those who are less fortunate.

In general, use an independent agent for any type of policy, as opposed to a representative of a single company, like Cigna or State Farm. The independent agent will show you policies from lots of different companies, just like a grocer who sells Snapple, Crystal Light, and Lipton iced teas.

HEALTH INSURANCE

Health care costs continue to rise faster than Oliver Stone can say *conspiracy*. Mom and Dad's policy used to cover you, and then there was the college infirmary. Now you're on your own, but you're young and strapping, right? So why worry when you can be happy?

For starters, even our age group should be covered. The going rate for a fractured finger, for example, is about $6,500, according to *Consumer Reports*. As for more serious injuries or illnesses that require hospital stays, the prices quickly run into the tens of thousands of dollars.

Second of all, now is the perfect time to find coverage, because virtually any insurance company will accept you. A young, healthy body is low-risk for them; meanwhile, you can lock yourself into a good plan. Remember, insurance is simply pooling risk to manage it; naturally, companies go to great lengths to limit the number of older and chronically ill policy-holders. The longer you wait to buy a health plan, the more difficult you will find it to be accepted.

Sure, if you procrastinate, there are plans that take anyone who applies. But common sense tells you that those plans will give you the least for your money, because they'll have so many claims to cover.

Finally, don't depend on your employer to have made the correct insurance decision for you. If you already have coverage and don't know what it covers and what it doesn't, take a deep breath and read the policy. It's a lot of fine print, but there are a few simple pointers. Here are a few terms to know:

Deductible: What you pay to the doctor before any insurance kicks in.

Co-pay: Your share of what the doctor is paid; the insurance company pays the balance of the bill.

Stop-loss: The most you could possibly pay in any one year.

COBRA: A federal law that allows you to keep your insurance for eighteen months when you either quit or are fired. You still have to pay for it; in fact, you pay the *full* cost of the policy plus a 2 percent surcharge. COBRA is basically a stall tactic, to give you a chance to find a new policy.

Keep in mind that *full* means not only your share, but *also* the employer's share, so be careful. For example, if you paid $100 a month for health insurance, and your company added $300 a month, you now have to pay around $400 to keep it.

The Basics

Carry your damn insurance card in your wallet. Let's face it: If the emergency room staffers know they'll be reimbursed, it's only common sense that they'll use every possible procedure to care for you. The medical system is no different from the justice system: Despite any ideals of equality, some schlump off the street gets a different sort of "justice" than William Kennedy Smith.

Want proof? A Harvard study of heart patients showed that patients with health insurance were 80 percent more likely to receive angiography, 40 percent more likely to get bypass grafting, 28 percent more likely to get angioplasty. Now granted, unless you're on the All-Butter Diet, you're not going to have a heart attack this young. But you get the point; money talks in a hospital.

As you research various plans, keep this in mind: The point is to protect yourself in the event of *major* injury or sickness. So get a policy that's "guaranteed renewable" or "conditionally renewable." Both mean that no matter how bad your health gets, the greedy insurance folks can't cancel your coverage. ("Conditionally" means that the only way they can cancel is if they void *all* of the same type of policies throughout the state; but *you* can never be singled out.)

There are two basic choices: fee for service or managed care. Once again, it's easiest to understand by example.

Fee for Service

It's Labor Day. Fall is in the air; you go hiking and mistake poison sumac for a raspberry bush. You develop a rash. Doc Holliday looks at it ($100), prescribes a cream ($30), and follows up in two weeks for another look ($70). All better for $200.

Soon, it's Halloween. You dress up as a family value (Murphy Brown), go to a party, compete in an intense game of beer pong, and fall off the second-story balcony into some shrubs below. You're whisked to the E.R. (where you wait for six hours), have your broken leg set ($900), stay the night for observation ($1,600), and, two months later, go to a dozen rehab appointments ($150 apiece)—for a grand total of $4,100.

In a fee-for-service plan, you might have a $300 deductible

and a 30 percent copay up to $3,000. So you pay for the rash, all $200, by yourself.

As for the leg, you start by forking over $100 to finish off the deductible. That leaves $4,000 owed. Then you pay 30 percent up to $3,000, which is $900, while the insurance company pays $2,100. That leaves $1,000 for the original $4,100 bill, which your plan covers all by itself. So you've paid $300 plus $900, or $1,200.

An HMO *(health maintenance organization)* provides *managed care*. The idea is that after a yearly fee, you pay only a few dollars per visit or per prescription. In return, you must use doctors who "participate" in the HMO.

In an HMO, for the rash, you'd pay $5 for each doctor visit, and $5 for the cream. The leg would cost you $50 for the hospital stay, and $5 times 12 visits—or $60—for the rehab. Your total: $15 plus $50 plus $60, or $135. Sounds like the HMO is perfect—but there are drawbacks, which we'll cover in a couple of paragraphs.

Some employers, usually corporate giants like General Motors, offer wonderful fee-for-service policies: they provide *first-dollar coverage*. That means you have no deductible. If so, great, but never spend your own money to buy such a policy. Employers usually offer these great plans only because of tax advantages and as wage trade-offs (that is, employees earn better health care instead of raises).

But the whole point of health insurance is really *last-dollar coverage*, where you're protected against the big risks—a spinal tear, a shattered tailbone, AIDS.

So you don't need insurance with a low deductible; the lower it is, the more expensive the policy. In choosing between, say, a deductible of $300 or $1,000, consider your past health—candidly. Some people are more injury-prone than others, because of fitness, diet, lifestyle (skiers beware), sexual activity, genetics, occupation, and a hundred other reasons. If you've needed a lot of medical care in the past, then you'd want the lower $300 deductible. If, however, you're generally healthy, pay less per month and accept the risk of a $1,000 deductible.

No matter what your plan, follow two rules of thumb: First, a *million-dollar* lifetime limit should be your *minimum*. I know it sounds absurd, but experts agree that half a million is too little for a lifetime.

Second, you need to check the financial rating (and see it on paper) of your insurer. Even some of the big, well-known companies are in financial trouble, and of course, some of the smaller ones are actually scams, fly-by-night companies that exist only on papers locked away in some Honolulu desk drawer. Any legitimate company can provide a copy of its credit rating from Duff and Phelps, Standard and Poor's, Moody's, or Best. Look for a rating of A, A+, AA, and the like. It's not like school, where a C means "average" or "fair." A C rating means trouble, and even Bs should give you pause. If the company folds around the time you fall off a cliff and fracture your tibia, you might not be covered.

Blue Cross and Blue Shield, however, don't have ratings. There are about 70 separate Big Blues, as they're known, for virtually every state and some cities. They were formed decades ago as nonprofit companies, combining their tax exemptions and volume discounts to provide affordable policies.

Lately, though, Blue Crosses and Blue Shields have been unstable. Because of their nonprofit mission, they accepted everyone who applied. The problem is that over the years, the healthiest people left the Big Blues and bought commercial insurance at lower prices. That left the Big Blues with the sickest clients and without enough healthy ones to spread the risk around.

As a result, most Big Blues have stopped open enrollments, and some have even given up their nonprofit status and become regular commercial companies with shareholders. Others have stayed the original course; steer clear of these, because your policy will go toward subsidizing the less healthy.

How do you know which Blue Crosses and Blue Shields are

in trouble? Over the past few years, *The Wall Street Journal* has reported that New Jersey, Rhode Island, New Hampshire, western New York, Massachusetts, New Mexico, Delaware, Maryland, and New York City Big Blues may not be financially sound. Virginia's, in fact, went bust (it ultimately merged with Ohio's). Obviously, the Big Blues of the Northeast are dangerous.

There are a host of things to check for when you read your fee-for-service policy: mental treatment, dental care, chiropractic, glasses, and prescriptions often aren't covered, which may well be okay with you. If you plan to have a baby, look carefully at maternity care; the trend is for insurers to pay for problems but not trouble-free deliveries—you may want a policy that provides "well-baby care" in the hospital and after birth. Also, note that surgery often requires advance written approval.

Carefully examine the Exclusions and Limitations section, which typically addresses preexisting conditions. These include anything that was treated (or should have been) within, say, the last six months before the date your coverage begins. Some companies make you wait to be treated for preexisting conditions; others won't pay for them, ever. I'm not a big fan of honesty, but tempting as it is to lie if you have a condition, know that your policy may be voided when you need it most.

Managed Care

You might wonder: Why have medical costs gone through the roof? For a long time, health insurance was structured so that patients felt they were spending other people's money—and they were. So any ache was cared for, every ailment was checked with expensive high-tech equipment. Doctors got rich.

You know what happened next—every college student who could stand the sight of blood and pass organic chemistry went to med school. My junior roommate, Tommy, was one of these people, and he and I cut a deal. Since I'm mathematically challenged, he did my calculus homework; since his literary skills rarely strayed beyond *Sports Illustrated,* I took care of his med school essays. I wrote that Tommy had "a burning desire to help humanity" and "to give back to the community," when all he really wanted was a Jaguar and sex with models.

But when Tommy graduated, he was carrying about $200,000 in loans and had no customers in sight. That's where managed care came in. The HMO offered Tommy a guaranteed pool of customers and thus a guaranteed income; Tommy, in turn, gave the HMO steep discounts on his services.

HMOs have become tremendously popular. Like fee-for-service plans, you pay a monthly fee, often $150 to $200 for a single person. But there's no deductible and usually only a nominal co-pay ($5, for example), so over time, HMOs are much cheaper. On the downside, your choice of doctors becomes limited; you have to use the HMO's doctors. That works in one of two ways: an HMO Central, which is an actual building filled with medical staff who all work for the HMO, or an HMO Local, which is basically a list of doctors who typically see some HMO patients and others with fee-for-service plans.

You get a primary-care physician, whom you see with any problem, from the flu to chronic back pain. She's the gatekeeper. She'll treat you herself or send you to a specialist (who also works for the HMO). One upside is that an HMO has an incentive to keep you healthy, which is good; they encourage annual physicals and preventive medicine. Better yet, there's almost no paperwork. On the downside, though, the HMO executives tend to pressure their doctors to keep expensive tests and procedures to an absolute minimum.

There are two views toward HMO quality: a cynical view and a benign one. The cynic would say, "Don't expect the same level of comfort and hand-holding in an HMO. Let's be honest: If these doctors were experienced top-of-the-liners, the absolute cream of the crop, they'd have lucrative private practices. Many doctors contract with HMOs because they want the customers, perhaps because their bedside manner isn't the most courteous, or they're young and less experienced, or they don't have the right social connections. Also, they're paid more per customer, so they just want to rush you through."

The benefactor would disagree. "HMOs are fine," he'd say. "You get a huge list of doctors, sometimes hundreds, to choose from. The majority of physicians participate in at least some type of HMO. There is still competition—if your doctor isn't courteous, rushes you, or doesn't seem to know what she's talking about, then you can always switch to another one within your plan. In addition, because the medical field attracts the best and brightest, and because the training is so demanding, virtually any doctor tends to be more than competent. And the plain reality is, even if you have a fee-for-service plan, you'd have a tough time finding out who the best doctors are, and an even tougher time getting an appointment. Especially for younger patients, who probably won't need complicated care (like cancer treatment), HMOs are a good bet."

You need to check the financial status of an HMO: Unlike a fee-for-service plan, it may not be rated. But you can look for a track record of at least three years, profitability, large enrollments, and at least part ownership by a corporation you've heard of, like Prudential or Cigna. Ask about price increases over the past three years; if they've been more than 12 percent annually, stay away.

One more thing: hybrid policies exist, too. That's what I own. When it comes to health, I'm paranoid enough to make Woody Allen look more stoic than Paul Bunyan. If I get into real trouble, I want the best fee-for-service doctor around. Meanwhile, however, I remain a starving writer, so I want cheap HMO coverage for all my minor flus and scrapes. Hybrids cost a bit more per month than either fee-for-service plans or HMOs by themselves, but they're perfect for the hypochondriac.

LIFE INSURANCE

At some point, within ten years of your high-school graduation, you will inevitably be contacted by an old classmate. He probably sat next to you in wood shop, went to all the pep rallies, was the first to purchase a class ring, and played tuba in the marching band—you know who I mean? We'll call him Herb.

Herb just got your phone number from your mom (bless her), and is calling to shamelessly push *whole-life* insurance on you. "Whole-life" should be loosely translated as "rip-off." Your reaction to Herb should be simple: hang up. The poor guy has been brainwashed, programmed with Branch Davidian-esque tenacity to believe he's actually selling you a good policy. Move over Hare Krishna, here comes Aetna.

In a 1994 Supreme Court decision, justices voted 8–1 that you may be very rude to Herb and his ilk, insult him, even give him a few strokes with the cane. Or at least they should have.

Whole-life insurance is a just short of a scam; it's certainly a bad deal. It combines two entities, insurance and investment, and sometimes a third—"dividends." Forget about "dividends": it means the insurers overcharge you for your policy and then give some of it back to you. Some deal.

As for the "investment" component—usually called the "savings" plan—your money would fare better in the bank, in a mutual fund, almost anywhere else. The returns are so low because the insurance company keeps so much for itself, then disguises its profits by confusing you with jargon and fancy accounting.

Herb will also explain, with great enthusiasm, that you can borrow against your policy. He'll even give you the rate in writing, right there in the policy. That's great. First "dividends" where they give you back your own money; now a "loan" where you pay for the privilege of *borrowing back* your own money.

Finally, the actual life insurance—you don't need it at your age. Not only are you extremely unlikely to die, but you probably don't have any dependents. Whom would you name as a beneficiary? Mom? Dad? The Elvis Presley estate? Whichever way, you're wasting your dough. You don't need life insurance until you have a family that depends on your income.

If you do have a kid or someone to support, consider *term-life* instead of whole-life. Herb probably won't mention term-life—which is the insurance component without the investment side—because it's much cheaper.

You might also consider disability insurance instead of life insurance. You are five and a half times more likely to be disabled for at least 90 days than you are to die before you retire. If you do have a risky lifestyle, buy a disability policy that would pay you 60 percent of your present pretax income.

APPLIANCE INSURANCE

A popular trend in electronics stores is to sell additional "store insurance," perhaps two years of parts-and-labor coverage for your new refrigerator. Don't buy it. There's typically a free manufacturer's warranty that covers the appliance at least past 90 days. If a big-ticket item is going to break early in its life, it'll happen within a few months. So save your money and skip the retailer's policy.

RENTER'S INSURANCE

You can protect your apartment from two orders of disaster: theft and damage. Damage could come from anything: a leaky roof, a fire, an earthquake, vandalism, and so on.

Should you purchase renter's insurance? That depends on four things:

1. Do you own a lot of valuables—jewelry, expensive stereo equipment, a mongo computer, cameras and camcorders, a large-screen TV? Do you live in a high-crime neighborhood?

2. How safe is your place itself? Are you meticulous about locking up? Are the windows barred? Do you use lights with a timer? Do you have sturdy locks? Do you have a doorman in your building? Are you on a high floor? Do you travel much?

3. Does your apartment complex have an insurance policy that you can piggyback on?

4. Is your area prone to weather disasters? Does the tenant above you have a Jacuzzi?

Remember that insurance is just a way to pool risks together. If your risks are small, you may be willing to take the chance on skipping insurance—maybe investing in better locks, then saving the difference.

If you do decide to buy renter's insurance, find out:

How large is the deductible?

Do you get reimbursed in full? Or will the company pay for a replacement? (See the following section.)

Are appliances depreciated? For example, a five-year-old fridge that originally cost $1,000 might get you only $500 if it's destroyed in a fire.

Are your roommates covered?

Replacement Value Versus Actual Value

If you do have things worth protecting, there are two routes toward buying insurance: the *replacement-value policy* and the (cheaper) *actual-value policy*. Say your Bose Surround Sound Acoustimass System, which you bought six years ago, is stolen. A replacement-value policy pays you the cost of a new, comparable system. An actual-value policy pays you what your six-year-old system would be worth if it were sold—in other words, even if your Bose system was in perfect condition, you might get only a fourth of what you paid for it in the first place.

Floater Policy

For jewelry, get a floater policy, which insures each individual piece. You might be able to ride on your parents' policy; ask. If not, you'll have the huge pain in the ass of assembling receipts for everything you own to match with any wreckage or police report.

How to File a Claim

First of all, you have to keep an inventory of what you own. You might mail it to family members in case of a fire or a robbery; you might even videotape your apartment. But ultimately, if you ever need to file a claim, you will probably need receipts or appraisals for all your belongings.

If it happens—if you start to push the key into the door and the door *falls* open—your heart will sink like a stone. It happened to me. I lived in a low-income part of Durham, North Carolina. I got home from Thanksgiving break to find my bike and my stereo gone. It really ticked me off because these guys took their time, snacked, drank a bottle of Jack Daniels, and made 900-number calls. In other words, they obviously weren't scared of my neighbors reporting them, which means they probably *were* my neighbors.

Your first step in any robbery is to file a police report. Resist the urge to neaten things up. Even if you figure they have no chance of catching the thief, call the cops and go through the paperwork.

After the cops are gone, you can set about repairing damage to locks, doors, and windows. If you discover the crime on a weekend and you can't reach your landlord, go ahead and pay the locksmith or window glazier yourself. The landlord should ultimately reimburse you, but even if that becomes a problem, your first priority is securing the apartment.

CAR INSURANCE

It's April 16, just after midnight. Cliffie is driving home from the post office—exhausted after a late night and all—and forgets to put on his headlights. As he makes a right turn, another car cuts him off. Cliffie smashes on the brakes, but too late—he's just run into Norm, going home after a big night at Cheers to celebrate the end of tax season. Is he covered? He has no idea.

You've got to pay attention when buying car insurance. It's easy just to sign up and assume you've got enough coverage when you don't. It's equally easy to get bamboozled into paying $500 or more a year for protection you don't need.

What You Need

Liability. This policy protects other people involved in an accident, not you. When you cause an accident, the insurance company pays for the victims' medical costs and any property damage. It also pays your legal fees and any civil court judgments that go against you. Make sure your liability covers you if you drive a friend's car (assuming you had her permission). Also, make sure it covers your friend if she drives *your* car.

Liability insurance is usually required by state law, but you can shop around for the best deal. You get to choose how much coverage you want. The agent, naturally, will try to scare you into buying lots of coverage. It's a tough call: How do you know whether you want $100,000 worth of protection or $500,000 worth of protection? As a rule of thumb, since you're young (and assuming you don't have a $1 million inheritance or any such large assets), you probably can get away with "100/300/100." That means your insurer will pay a maximum of $100,000 for medical expenses to any one victim of your negligence; not more than $300,000 for medical expenses of all the victims of your negligence; and not more than $100,000 for any property damage you cause.

Collision. With this type of insurance, you're protected against damage caused to your car. The insurer will pay to fix or replace your car. Unlike liability insurance, in most states you don't need to get collision protection. But should you?

If your car is less than five years old, or it's leased, you should probably buy it. To keep the rates down, keep the deductible high. You're protecting yourself against being totaled, not against a fender-bender. In other words, you'll pay a lower annual insurance rate if you accept the Policy B $1,000 deductible rather than the Policy A $500 deductible. The flip side is that if your car is vandalized and you need a $1,000 paint job, Policy B will pay you just $100—you'll have to cover the rest. Policy A, on the other hand, will pay you $600 toward the repair.

Comprehensive. This policy protects against everything from theft to terrorism. Forget it.

Options. Insurance companies offer items like a "free" rental car or "free" towing as options. If you already belong to AAA or some auto club, you can skip the towing option. But the rental car can be useful. Even moderate damage takes a few days to repair (auto shops are like doctors' waiting rooms), and a rental can cost from $50 to $100 per day. So if the rental car option costs five or ten bucks, go with it. But since your chances of being in an accident and needing that rental car are small, don't pay much more than that.

Medical insurance. This might be offered as an option, but it's probably covered on your health plan. Get a copy of the auto plan's medical coverage from the car insurance agent, then show it to your health insurance agent. If possible, get the health insurance agent to sign a one-sentence note saying you're covered for it. Note that your health care plan does not cover your passengers if you cause an accident, but your liability insurance does.

Shopping for the Best Rates

Here, your age is already working against you in a big way. Being young, you're more of a risk to be an aggressive driver. If you're male, you're even more likely to crank it up to 110 mph. The result is that car insurance costs hundreds of dollars more for the under-30 age bracket. The rates will be even higher if you have any speeding tickets on your record, or if you live in a city (more crime, more accidents). Don't try to register in your parents' hometown, either, to get out of paying a higher "city" premium. Insurers will do anything to get out of paying a claim once you're actually in an accident. So if you write down a home address of Krumsville, Pennsylvania, and your car gets smashed in Washington, D.C., the claims officer will probably investigate.

You might get discounts on your rates if:

- Your car has air bags, antilock brakes, or certain antitheft devices.
- You have good college grades.
- You take a driver's ed. course.
- You carpool regularly.
- You use public transportation to get to work.
- You pay the whole year's premium at once.
- You don't drink.

But the biggest discount you can get is for *not* buying a flashy car. Insurers have realized that people who buy Iroc-Z's tend to have leaden feet. For any of these discounts, you simply need to ask your insurer—sometimes more than once.

Accidents

They happen. When they do, become a reporter: Get any names and numbers you can—license plate numbers, descriptions of vehicles, time of day, the exact circumstances, witnesses, even witnesses' descriptions and license plate numbers. Get the names of the cops who come. Ask to see the driver's license of whoever was at the wheel of the other car and offer yours at the same time. Ask to see his or her insurance card. *Insist.* Naturally, people are hostile in this situation. Some of them (illegally) don't have insurance. Some are more worried about their rates going up, especially if they're driving a clunker that one more dent won't hurt.

When you get home, begin the claims process right away. Every time you deal with an agent, get that person's name, first and last, and his or her direct extension. Ask if that person will be shepherding the claim through. Ask when you can expect to have the claim completed and repeat the information back, the way you do when it's clear that you're writing it down. ("Joe . . . Agent A-G-E-N-T . . . says . . . process . . . done . . . by . . . November . . . 8th.")

Ask whether you can call again in three days to check on the status of your claim. Ask what time is convenient for the agent. Mark it in your calendar. Be a pain in the ass: In the car insurance world especially, the squeaky wheel gets the grease.

chapter four

Those Fleeting Two Weeks

TRAVEL TIPS

You're an adult now. No more summer vacations trekking across Europe or camped out on the beach. No more spring break packages in ramshackle hotels along Daytona Beach. From now on, your vacations will come in short bursts. Plus, you may be traveling for a whole new reason: work. You're getting too old for hostels, sleeping bags, park benches, and hotel room floors. You're ready to pay. On business, smooth logistics can make the difference between success and failure—a missed wake-up call, a lumpy mattress, a broken air conditioner, or a canceled flight all can mean being late, unkempt, or just exhausted for that all-important meeting. Similarly, if you're really going to enjoy those measly two weeks of vacation a year, it pays to plan. Nothing sours a vacation more than worrying about whether you should have bought collision insurance, griping over the exchange rate, or fuming over a hotel that ripped you off.

All travel fees are based on a simple principle: Business travelers aren't too worried about the cost, since they're not paying. That's why flying first class costs at least double the economy rate and why hotel and car-rental rates plummet if you'll stay over on Saturday night. If you use this principle to your advantage, you'll save a bundle on all your excursions.

How to Find a Travel Agent

No shock here: try to get a recommendation, and shop around. The basic requirements include being certified and having a computer reservation system. APOLLO, DATAS II, SABRE, and System One are the big ones. Then look for personal knowledge: Do they know the basics about no-fee travelers' checks, where visas are needed, where to exchange currency? Can they tell you about other clients' experiences in the same part of the world?

Next, you need someone willing to make ten calls on your behalf to find the best rate and to keep on top of it, since rates change all the time. Is the agent already superbusy, someone who will want to get your travel plans executed as fast as possible with the least effort? How fast does she deliver your plane tickets? By messenger? Does her firm have 24-hour service in case of catastrophe? Does it have affiliates in other cities? Does the agency have a deal with a consolidator, which is essentially a wholesaler of discount airplane and cruise-line tickets? Similarly, do they have a deal with a hotel booking service, which offers discount rates at hotels?

All the travel agent's services should be free. They make money by charging commissions, which are almost always paid by the seller, not by you. For example, a round-trip Minneapolis-to-Dallas flight would cost you $355 whether you reserved directly through American Airlines or through your travel agent; the agent might earn $30 of that $355 from American. Keep in mind that the "free" system may not be what it seems. It can work against you: If Huey Cruise Lines pays the agent $100 commission, he might recommend them over Dewey Cruise Lines, which offers only a $50 commission, even though Dewey has a better package and would be cheaper for *you*. If you live in a small town, you might call an agency in the nearest large city; they're typically more competitive, which means lower prices.

Finally, you want an experienced agent. He should know that southern Turkey is politically unstable; that some Arab nations won't let you in if your passport has an Israeli stamp; that May in Ecuador is unbearable; that you need a visa to enter Russia but not to enter Hungary; and which inoculations you need before visiting Cameroon. He should be aware that the Sun Valley resort you picked out of a brochure is in bankruptcy and customers have complained about shoddy service, or that the Holiday Inn in San Francisco charges five bucks extra for every long-distance call. He should warn you that jellyfish are rampant this summer in Wildwood, New Jersey, or that your would-be relaxing golf-and-tennis vacation at Myrtle Beach coincides with spring break at the University of South Carolina.

A Traveler Recalls: Keep a Copy of Your Passport

"I was waiting in the train station in Amsterdam, in line to buy a ticket," Brendan recalls. "You might say I was a little, um, out of it. Anyway, my passport was stolen. I was heading to France, but it was too late to go to the French consulate, since they keep these ridiculously short hours—you know, like 2:00 P.M. to 2:45 P.M. The rest of the day is lunch. When I finally got to the consulate the next day, it took forever, because I was short on paperwork."

MORAL: When traveling abroad, keep a photocopy of your passport separate from the passport itself. It'll save you a lot of headaches if you lose the original.

Ask your agent the conditions under which you may cancel a trip that you want to book. She may guarantee a refund if you cancel for valid reasons or explain that cancellation has a slight penalty. You'd better ask what *valid* and *slight* mean. After all, to George Foreman, 230 pounds is slight and an occasional pop in the face is valid. It's not uncommon in the real world for a boss to suggest that you delay your vacation for a few weeks, and you don't want to be stuck.

Packing

Soft suitcases are light but offer less protection than the regular kind. Suitcases on wheels have taken over the luggage industry in the past couple of years; just make sure you don't skimp in this area, because cheapo wheels jam up after a few trips, and you'll end up dragging, rather than rolling, the case. Even simpler are those little metal fold-up pullcarts, on which you can place a couple of regulation suitcases.

Try not to buy luggage new. Get it used—at garage sales, in your parents' attic, from classified ads. The nicer the suitcase's appearance, the more likely a criminal will decide that you're rich, and thus the more likely that it will be stolen.

Travel light rather than anticipate every possible situation. You don't need a different pair of shoes for each outfit; you don't need to take a sportcoat *and* a suit; you don't need to take a ski parka, a raincoat, and a windbreaker. Packing light makes the worst part of travel—the airports, cabs, and so on—more bearable.

But how to pack light? Pick lightweight, dark, color-coordinated, low-maintenance fabrics. A black cotton-knit shirt, for example, will conceal dirt, won't wrinkle, can be worn with any pants and shoes, is comfortable in any weather, and doesn't weigh much.

Once your gear is set aside, (1) get rid of a third of it; (2) stretch shirts the length of the suitcase and fold them at the seams; (3) halve pants, then halve them again into squares; (4) put shoes along the sides, with a pair of socks in each shoe; (5) shove your underwear around to even things out; (6) stuff additional socks into the corners; and (7) tuck everything in with a towel or shawl to be clear of zippers.

Finally, here's a lightweight tip: Line your suitcase with

plastic trash bags. They weigh nothing, they protect your belongings from dampness in airplane luggage compartments, and
they will keep your dirty clothes from piling on the floor, hold
a wet bathing suit, or separate your clean clothes from the dirty
on the trip home. This way, you can just put the unused clothes
right back in your dresser when you return home.

What You'll Forget	
For skiing	Sock liners, sunglasses, lip balm, suntan lotion, aspirin.
For camping	Insect repellent, hat, antiseptic, flashlight, towels.
For the beach	Sweatshirt for chilly nights and to cover sunburn, aloe, Solarcaine, aspirin, flip-flops, bathing suit cover-up.

Flying

Airplane tickets are like gasoline: Despite what the airlines and
oil companies claim, all flights are essentially the same. Sure,
just as the oil companies offer you a credit card, a convenience
store, super octane, gasoline detergents, and those little Hess
truck toys, the airlines also try to distinguish themselves with
extra-perky flight attendants, saltier peanuts, wider seats,
claims of more on-time arrivals. But most people base their
flight decisions on one simple factor: What'll it cost?

What we have in the airline business, then, is pretty close
to perfect competition. If Delta offers a coach fare from New
York to Los Angeles for $250, you can bet that any other major
carrier will be priced between $230 and $270. This makes it
hard to shop around for better prices, because there usually *are*
no better prices.

That is, prices are roughly the same from airline to airline.
You *can* get discounts, however. The most basic price break, of
course, is the *advance purchase*, which usually comes in the

form of 7-day, 14-day, or 21-day. These dates have a way of sneaking up on you, so once you know you're ready to travel, jump on the phone and make the reservation. Another rate to ask about is the excursion fare, which has a minimum and maximum stay. The idea here is that if you're a business traveler, you won't stay a day more than necessary. (Remember that the goal of the airline is to give discounts to vacationers but not to business people.)

G.I.T. is *group-inclusive travel,* a rate for traveling with a group that you might not need to be part of. Then there are *super-saver fares,* which are simply a few cheap tickets set aside by the airline for each flight. The airlines like super-savers because they get to advertise them and get people excited about traveling, even though the ultralow rates disappear quickly and most people get offered only the 7-day advance rates. (A side note: Ticket prices in newspaper and magazine ads are usually for one-way based on round-trip, so read the fine print.) And just because you're out of college doesn't mean you can't get a youth fare. They're often good until you're 26 years old. Finally, keep calling for fares! The price today can often be significantly cheaper than last week.

Make sure you compare rates for any nearby airports. Let's say, for example, that you're an engineer who needs to get from Chapel Hill to Detroit for your job interview with Chrysler. Flying from Raleigh-Durham International Airport to Detroit might be $100 more expensive than a flight from Greensboro Airport to Detroit. Sure, it'll take an extra hour to drive to Greensboro. But a hundred bucks will certainly more than pay for the extra time and gas.

An important note on airplane lingo. *Direct* is not the same as *nonstop.* Direct flights can land in other cities (though you won't switch planes). Nonstops are simply *A* to *B.* Sometimes you *want* a stopover, because you can get a free stay. For example, you can fly New York to Tel Aviv nonstop, or you can fly direct, changing planes in London. They cost about the same. But your direct ticket might allow you to land in London on a Tuesday, poke around the pubs for a few days, then continue your flight to the Holy Land on Thursday without any additional cost.

Recently, there has been a large expansion in "discount" airlines. These carriers, like Midway, Republic Air, and ValuJet, don't fly nearly as many routes as the major airlines. They usually are light on the amenities—no meals, perhaps, or less-fluffy pillows. The planes are a bit older. Most don't offer frequent flyer miles. Some discount airlines even save money by eliminating paper tickets (everything is kept in the computer). But the savings can be huge. An Atlanta–Dallas ticket, which might go for $300 on a major carrier, might be had for $170 on ValuJet.

There are drawbacks. Often there are reservation restrictions, where you can't purchase a ticket more than, say, seven days in advance. If a Midway flight is canceled for mechanical reasons, then, unlike a giant carrier like American, there might not be another plane available for an entire day. And there are, of course, safety considerations. But the FAA has been far more diligent in policing these value airlines since the ValuJet crash in the Everglades.

FARE WARS

For the past several years, airlines have been waging fare wars. These wars are the result of deregulation during the 1980s and won't continue forever. But for now, enjoy the prices—watch your Sunday paper for advertised specials. Usually, the phone lines jam on the same day the ad runs, so contact a travel agent, who can usually book through a computer. Travel agents are paid commissions by the airline, so you have no additional expense.

If you miss a "sale" reservation deadline by only a few hours—whether it's a seven-day advance ticket or some super-saver, limited-time-only deal—you can still beat the system. Call a travel agent in a more western time zone; that is, if you're in

Orlando, call an agent in California or even Hawaii. If you missed the deadline by a day or two, *still* call your travel agent; often he can "backdate" tickets for you, even though he's not supposed to.

You've always wondered about your Sunday paper's Travel section: What are those small ads in microscopic fonts that list *über-cheap* prices for international destinations? They're called *consolidators*. They're low-profile wholesalers. They buy blocks of discounted tickets from the airlines, sometimes chartering entire flights. In turn, they sell seats to travel agencies and to consumers directly.

These can be terrific deals, but be wary: some are (pardon the pun) fly-by-night operations. Make that call to the Better Business Bureau and pay with a credit card. Also, find out if they have the right to cancel or change price or itinerary. Some of them reserve this right in case a group cancels. For example, say Mongo Travel typically buys 10 extra seats for a group of 50; in other words, the 50 is already contracted—maybe by the local Rotary club—so Mongo tries to pick up a few extra bucks by buying 60 seats from Delta at their superlow group rate, then selling the 10 seats at a profit. If Mongo gets rid of only, say, 7 of those 10 seats, they'll still make money. But what if the Rotary club cancels? Then Mongo might decide to give back their whole block of 60 seats to Delta. You do get a refund, but you also end up stranded, without a flight. Still, once the consolidator actually sends you an airline ticket, you're safe—that ticket cannot be invalidated.

Two of the larger consolidators are STA Travel (800-777-0112) and Fare Deals (800-347-7006). (If these numbers are no longer in use when you call, remember that 800-555-1212 is the number for toll-free directory assistance.)

WHERE TO SIT

Most people prefer either the window or the aisle—if you use a travel agent, she should keep your preferences on file. The experts say that airplanes are considered marginally safer in the back. Why? In a crash, the nose of the plane is more likely to hit the ground first. If the plane is in an accident on the ground, the biggest danger is usually that the fuselage will catch fire. Still, the difference in safety is not so great that you should pay a lot of attention to it.

A Passenger Recalls a Near Miss

Joe Stevenson once had to make an emergency evacuation from a DC-9 flight. "I panicked a little bit. I never listened to the safety presentation—does anyone? I just didn't want to even think about the possibility that I'd need to know anything about crashes." Joe's "crash" wasn't all that bad—though several people were injured, almost all injuries were minor, and Joe himself escaped with a bump on the head and a scrape when he went down the slide. "It was kind of chaotic, because even though the flight attendants were calm, a lot of the passengers on that flight didn't speak English. I skinned my arm on the slide; now I wear long sleeves when I travel, even in the summer. They tell you to leave everything, but of course everyone was grabbing purses and briefcases and backpacks. It was actually kind of a crazy scene, and I'm glad there weren't more passengers aboard."

MORAL: It might happen to you one day, and there's not much you can do about a crash besides wearing comfortable clothing (no heels, especially) and occasionally listening to the safety briefing.

American Airlines was the safest carrier in a 1993 report by the International Airline Passengers Association. USAir had a very tough 1994 and 1995, with a few accidents leading to an FAA investigation. Still, USAir and all the major American carriers, such as TWA, Northwest, Continental, Delta, and United, have excellent records. And the big-name midsize airlines are safe, too, like America West and Southwest, which, as of mid-1995, had *never* had an accident. You've got to look out for some of the foreign airlines, though. While you'll remember from Dustin Hoffman in *Rain Man* that Australia's "Qantas never crashed," India's and Columbia's airlines are atrocious. The risk is worse flying *within* those nations, from city to city. That is, New York to New Delhi on Air India is okay, but be careful about New Delhi to Calcutta on some domestic Indian carrier. These unregulated airlines sometimes lack even navigational equipment, so pilots might not even know where they are!

IN-FLIGHT COMFORT

To stay comfortable during takeoff and landing, chew gum or candy—anything to keep you swallowing, which constantly recalibrates the inner pressure on your ear. Be careful about holding your nose and forcing air against your middle ear. That can puncture an eardrum. Use decongestant and nose spray if you're flying with a cold, but beware—it will still be painful. Realize that the cabin is *very* dry and drink as many fluids as you can—not alcohol, though, which is itself dehydrating, nor coffee, which is a diuretic. If you do kick back with a few beers, try to drink lots of water, too. (Also, try to get an aisle seat, if you know what I mean.)

EMERGENCY

Once, just once, you should pay attention to the "In case of . . ." presentation at the beginning of the flight. One item that they don't prepare you for: If the pilot and crew suddenly die, walk into the cockpit, tune the radio to 121.5, and say "Mayday." Repeat as needed.

"I was in O'Hare Airport, listening to Alice in Chains on my Walkman," says Alvin Tolbert, "when this old lady beside me nudged me. 'A young fellow like yourself should take advantage of this opportunity,' she said. I started to edge away, thought she was one of those weird religious people, but she told me, 'They're giving away $200 in travel credits if you volunteer to get bumped.' Hey. I'd already been traveling for about eighteen hours, and I'd slept the last night in a very uncomfortable chair at Dulles Airport in Washington. I was extra cranky because all the bars at Dulles had closed at 10 P.M., right in the middle of *Monday Night Football.* I just wanted to get home. Still, $200 in credits wasn't bad. So I went up and volunteered. It was well worth it. I waited another three hours, but they flew me first class. Let me tell you about first class—you're a writer, so you'll never know what it's like. Mmm, those seats—bigger, wider, more comfortable, leather. Man, they pamper you up there. I had five free drinks. They kiss your ass. If you're asleep they'll sneak beside you and close the blinds. It's really great."

MORAL: When traveling around holiday season, ask when you check in whether there might be a possibility that you could volunteer to be bumped. And keep your Walkman low so you can hear important announcements. Or sit next to a very nice old lady whom you can trust to tell you about exciting opportunities to give up your seat. Just make sure she's not a religious freak.

CANCELED FLIGHTS

If your flight is canceled, the major airlines have reciprocal agreements in which tickets are honored on other carriers. So if Continental's flight has technical problems, they'll often be able to get you on the American flight an hour later. If the flight is overbooked (which is common in December), then the attendant or pilot may offer to bump someone from a seat. Usually, the person bumped gets the next flight and some bonus—maybe $100 off your next airline ticket, maybe a *free* trip, maybe a hotel and dinner if the next flight isn't until tomorrow. But the deal might not be as sweet as it seems—$30 for dinner sounds like plenty, except the deal is usually good only for the hotel restaurant, where an entrée alone might go for $25.

If you're late for a flight (within two hours or so), most airlines will put you on the next available one. If you're several hours late, and most of the flights are booked, you need a good excuse. This isn't like school; a note from Mom isn't enough. Most airlines want something official, like a doctor's note, or an arrest certificate from the sheriff's office saying they'd been holding you for murder (that gets any airline official's attention). If you can't come up with any of these, bribe a doctor to write a note saying you were sick, go to the airport, concoct a story, and stick to your guns. Insist on speaking to the manager. Don't give up. Nobody can afford to eat a $400 ticket. In the end, they'll probably just sock you with a "new-ticket fee" or some such nonsense, which will set you back $50 or so. But what the hell were you doing to be more than two hours late for a flight? Oh. That.

AIR COURIER

You may have heard of "air courier" deals—round-trip to London for $100, Hong Kong for $200—and probably wondered: What do you have to do, carry large bags of heroin? No! They're mostly documents. It's a dyslexic fee plan—the later you reserve, the *lower* the rate. You sometimes can't get frequent flyer miles, but on the upside, if the airline loses your luggage, who cares?

Air couriers give up some of their baggage to companies needing to ship time-sensitive cargo. You fly on a regular airline. You just have to travel light, be flexible in scheduling, and be willing to travel solo.

Companies use couriers (rather than simply shipping their stuff as freight) because it's quicker. Freight has to be at an airport around five hours before takeoff; you, the passenger, can be there as late as a half hour before departure. And as much as you complain about it, your baggage comes off the plane within 30 minutes of when you land; freight often takes twelve hours to be fully unloaded. The real sticker, however, is customs: Freight can take a few *days* to clear.

This isn't brain surgery. You call the courier company and say, "Hi, what's available for flights from New York to Berlin in September?" They want to book you as soon as possible, to make sure they've got someone locked in. So they'll want money right away. Some will accept deposits; some will accept credit cards (for additional fees); some want certified checks; some want you to pay in person.

They maintain the right to bump you, though that's rare. On flight day, you'll meet a rep at the airport. Only then will you get your ticket. The rep might be late, so bring the company's phone number so you can hassle them until he shows up.

He'll give you a one-way ticket, instructions for your return, and a sheaf of cargo documents. Then he'll walk you through check-in. You probably won't even see the items that you're transporting; you certainly won't touch them. The rep will check them in. You may be given the baggage-claim stubs, however.

Upon arrival, there are two ways to meet your rep: either you'll hold up the envelope of cargo documents (which are clearly labeled), or you'll have a phone number to call. Once you make contact, you'll wait in customs while the courier company rep deals with all the paperwork. Then you're free to go. That's it! The return flight is the same routine—you'll call a local courier rep the day before your scheduled departure to make sure there haven't been any changes to your ticket (you may be told to take an earlier or later flight).

Here are some courier companies, though their phone numbers may have changed, or they may even have gone out of business before press time:

Now Voyager—212-431-1616

Discount Travel International—212-362-3636

Air Tech—212-219-7000

Halbart—718-656-8279

Rental Cars

A good rental-car agent, if she's doing her job, is trying to squeeze an extra $50 to $100 out of you. To hold on to your money, you've got to know what to look for. Unlimited mileage is usually standard. Unfortunately, so is a minimum age of 25. A few chains will rent their cars to us younger folk, but they usually tack on a king-sized surcharge—$30 a day in some cases. If you're young enough to be in this high-risk group, ask about the surcharge when you reserve. Otherwise, the agent might forget to mention it until you're all ready to pick up the car, and then it's too late. After all, what's your alternative when the rental agent knows that every other renter in town has a 25-years-old minimum? Ride a bike?

When you pick up the phone to reserve a car, keep in mind that the agents don't volunteer the best rates. You have to press to get special deals. If you see an advertised discount, clip it out. Then reserve with the ad in front of you. There's usually a code, which the agent may need for the computer. That seems to be the modus operandi of these car agencies— they make it difficult for you to redeem your discounts, then blame it on the computer—"My screen is not showing the rate you claim."

YOU CAN GET DISCOUNTS FOR:

- Weekend rates are usually good for noon Thursday to noon Monday. Beware. If you're late in returning, the company might charge you the weekday rate for *each* day you rented the car. In other words, if you come in at 1 P.M. on Monday, they may try to charge you the higher weekday rate for not only that Monday, but Saturday and Sunday, too.

- A variation on the weekend rate is the Saturday night stay-over. As the name implies, you must keep the car for Saturday night. Hertz, Avis, and the rest assume that if you're on business, you'd prefer to return the car and get home, rather than waste the weekend just to get a good rate. Customers who want a car for Saturday night, therefore, are usually tourists or vacationers, and more price-sensitive than business types.

- Members of AAA and other auto clubs often get small discounts, typically somewhere around 10 percent, for showing their membership cards. If you have time before you leave on a trip and need maps, call your local AAA and ask for their "Triptiks." These are easy-to-manage maps that a AAA staff member will personally highlight to mark the best route for you, avoiding construction and other problem roads. Of course, you have to be a member—it costs around $40 or so per year, which includes emergency services like free towing. If you need those services, only one person in the car has to be a member—not necessarily the driver.

- Your long-distance company, American Express, Visa, airlines, and other companies all offer coupons for discounts on rental cars. The coupons usually come in the mail with your bills or statements. Try to save those coupons, because they're usually long-term offers and the discounts can be significant.

AT THE RENTAL-CAR COUNTER

The agent will try to bump you to a bigger car. Unless you're ferrying a visiting sumo team, say no. He may then contend that the local conditions make a subcompact a bad choice. ("You might have some problems getting to Philly, all those hills, with that little four-cylinder engine.") Shoot back: "If your cars don't get the job done, why do you rent them?" Then stick to your game plan, unless you're in the Himalayas or other rugged terrain.

INSURANCE

Insurance is a big profit-maker for Hertz, Avis, Budget, and all the rest. The agent will definitely try to sell you a collision- or loss-damage waiver (CDW or LDW). This is in case someone damages or steals the car. You probably don't need CDW from the rental agent, if you have (a) your own car insurance and/or (b) American Express, Diner's Club, Visa Gold or MasterCard Gold, or other credit cards. Before you leave on a trip, make that one call to your insurer to find out if the policy for your car at home extends to a rental car. Even at the rental office, you can call the customer service number on the back of your credit card (assuming you're going to pay for the car with that card!). If you're already covered, why pay Hertz for duplicate insurance?

If you are relying on CDW from your credit card, keep in mind that one common limitation is time. Most credit cards cover maximum rental spans of between two weeks and 31 days. After that, you're no longer covered. So if you need a car for two months, check carefully before waiving the CDW. Also, the Discover card is a special case. While Visa and American Express usually offer the insurance for free, Discover charges you a $7 fee for car rental insurance. Discover also will not cover car rentals outside the U.S.A. and Canada.

The rental agent will not be pleased if you waive her CDW

insurance pitch. She may say, "We don't have an agreement with Visa, so we don't honor that." This is an outright *lie*. The Visa deal is with *you*, not with the rental car company. Liability insurance is different. This covers when *you* damage someone else's car. If you don't own your own car, you probably need to buy this from the rental agent. It should cost somewhere around $8 a day for $1 million in coverage.

If you do have your own car at home, then your liability insurance should cover rental cars, too. But you certainly need to ask your insurance agent at home. Also, your annual insurance rates would skyrocket if you did cause an accident, whereas if you buy the rental agency's LDW, even an accident that was your fault wouldn't be reported to your insurance agency. So if you plan to do some reckless driving, buy Hertz's LDW. Otherwise, make sure you're already covered, and skip the waiver.

Finally, there's *redlining,* a relatively new addition to car-renting scams. This is where a rental-car agency marks off an area whose local residents must pay a surcharge to cover "vicarious liability"—which is legalese for people suing the *rental-car company* if they get hit, in addition to suing the driver. Some areas have a lot more of these vicarious liability claims, based on the combination of local driving culture and on the concentration of aggressive ambulance-chasing lawyers. So the companies redline those areas, which is a sort of legal discrimination.

For example, a Hertz office in New York City may charge a Bronx resident upwards of $50 per *day* extra to rent a car, while someone with an out-of-state license would get the regular rate for the same car from the same branch. So if you need to rent a car locally—whether you don't have your own and need to go out of town, or because your car is in the shop, or whatever—and the quoted rate sounds really high, ask if the area is redlined for local residents. If so, it may make sense to take a bus to a rental agency that's farther away but doesn't redline.

YOUR DRIVING RECORD

Hertz, Budget, and Avis may check your driving record. They get their information from the state DMV. Each company has its own rules. They may, for example, reject you if you've had even a single accident within the past four years which caused any bodily injury. This is legal. So if you have a bad driving record, you could be out of luck.

RETURNING THE CAR

If for any reason you suspect the rental agent of being a bit fishy or underhanded, when you return the car you may want to ask to sign off on damage to the car.

You'll probably be given a full tank of gas (check the gauge when you first get into the driver's seat) and you're supposed to return the car with the same amount. If the car's not filled up, they'll charge you an outrageous price for the gas, sometimes 25 percent or more over the price at the local service station. If you've got a companion, beware of fees for extra drivers. Do not try to hide the extra drivers: If you get into an accident and your friend is driving, you're screwed. Also, when calling to reserve a car, ask about *drop-off charges* if you need to pick it up in, say, Santa Fe but want to return the car in a nearby city like Albuquerque, of if you want to pick up a car at La Guardia Airport and return it at JFK (both of which are in the New York City metropolitan area). The drop-off fee is supposed to compensate them for having to send the car back to its original home. *One-way rentals* can also be convenient; most large companies will offer them (and charge you, too). "One-way" means picking up the vehicle in one city and returning it in another one that's far away, like if you're moving all your belongings out of your Ann Arbor dorm and back to Oklahoma City.

CREDIT CARD HOLDS

These are a pain in the neck. Many companies will *hold* $2,000 or more on your card. That means they'll reserve money against your limit, especially when you're abroad, in case their car is damaged. Some companies might hold less if you buy their CDW. Since many cards have $1,000 limits, your spending might be locked up entirely by one credit card hold. That means you wouldn't be able to use your Visa for anything else you might want to buy, like, say, dinner.

Ask *before* you make your reservation how much they hold against your card. And, as in all important phone conversations, get the first and last name of the person you speak to. It's a lot more convincing to say, "I spoke to your employee Del Unser on February 12 and he told me you'd only hold $500 on my card, and that's why I chose your company," than to say, "That's not what I was told over the phone." If you *do* get stuck with a large hold, it helps to have two cards; put the car on American Express and use your Visa for that Aztec-temple-ruin-adobe-pottery thing you think your Aunt Edna would love.

If You're Driving Your Own Car

Before you take any long trips, a mechanic should look at your spark plugs, ignition timing, brakes, and choke, according to the AAA. In addition to helping prevent any major problems, you'll save a few bucks on fuel. The air filter should be changed twice a year; the battery should be free of corrosion; the belts should not be frayed. If the oil has not been changed in the last three months, do it before you go.

You can check the tires yourself. Place the gauge over the valve, press down, and read the number on the little plastic stick that shoots out. Compare that pressure to the suggested pressure in the manual, and fill accordingly; you'll get better gas mileage. While you're down there squatting around the tires, check out the tire threads. If they're worn down evenly, get new tires. If they're worn unevenly, have a mechanic check the car's wheel balance, alignment, and suspension.

Check oil level, coolants, and fluids for the transmission, brakes, and power steering. See if there are any extras in the trunk you can unload to make the car lighter. Take the opportunity to pull the spare tire out of the car (yes, it's heavy) and check its air pressure, too. Don't expect a spare to sit on the bench for five years *and* be ready to play on demand (that is, when you get a flat).

AAA is the best known auto club (it's not-for-profit). Others include the National Automobile Club (based in L.A.), the U.S. Auto Club (based in Dallas), and those of the oil companies (Texaco, Shell, Exxon, Chevron, Amoco, and so on).

Hotels

Checking into a hotel is the final stage of a negotiation. Unfortunately, most people don't treat it as such, and simply pay what they're told at the end of the stay. The fact is that front desk clerks have the power to offer lower rates; you just need to know what to ask for. Usually they are instructed not to offer you any deals, but if you hang in there long enough and pester them about discounts, they commonly come across with one of the 1,001 various deals they have going. The most common discount is the *corporate rate* (The front desk may ask for a business card to give you that rate.)

The first stage of the negotiation occurs over the phone. Here you have the most power. The Hilton people know that once you're physically at their hotel, you're probably tired, and unlikely to go to the Sheraton just to save a few bucks. But over the phone, *you* have the power. The Sheraton is just an 800 call away, and the Hilton knows this. So if you bug him long enough, the reservation clerk might suddenly realize, "Oh, the computer just showed a supersaver rate," and give you a sweet deal.

Once you agree on a price, get a written confirmation sent to you, or get a reservation number over the phone. Prices are usually for double occupancy, either per *room* or per *person*. Find out which. There should be no extra charge if you want two single beds instead of a double. If you're a total loser and must travel alone, there is usually a supplemental price for single occupancy. In other words, instead of charging you half of the double-occupancy rate, they might only knock a couple of dollars off. So ask if there's a supplemental charge for single occupancy. You might convince them to waive it as long as you bring up the issue over the phone. Finally, always ask what extras are included. Free parking? Ice? A continental breakfast? A backrub? (Unlikely.)

The negotiation is not over when you hang up. Call back tomorrow at a different time; try to get an even better rate. If yesterday you reserved a room for $50 at the Sheraton, call today and tell them that your boyfriend reserved a room for $40 at the nearby Hilton—will they match that price? Bluff.

Discounters

There are several companies that specialize in booking rooms at a discount. They operate like consolidators do with airlines: Because they deal in large quantities, the hotel chains give them superlow rates. Part of the savings is passed on to you.

Travel Planners (800-221-3531) is one of the best services. Often, they'll get you half price on rooms at major hotels, like Marriott, Best Western, Sheraton, and so on. Hotel Reservation Network (800-964-6835) does the same thing. Campus Travel (800-525-6633) offers universities worldwide that rent cheap rooms. Entertainment Publications (800-477-3234) is a bit different: Like Travel Planners, they can get you half-price rooms in thousands of hotels. You need to pay a fee, though, to be a member.

Upon arrival, try for an even lower price. You've got nothing to lose. Also, many hotels have business suites for the same price as single rooms, which can be had for the same price you already agreed on if they aren't occupied. After all, the hotel wants to make you happy (at least in theory), and it's no extra cost to them to give you a larger room. Again, ask.

Foreigners

Each nation has its own verbal and nonverbal ways of communicating. We Americans find silence awkward; other cultures appreciate it. We tend to speak directly and look the person we're speaking to in the eye; in some nations, people hedge and look away as a matter of respect (which we'll deride as shifty-eyed). Tell a Korean man to give you a yes-or-no answer and you'll probably get *yes*, even if in his heart the true answer is *no*. Thais don't even have a word for *no*. To the contrary, in addition to having poor taste in music and movies, the French have the annoying habit of saying *no* when they mean *maybe*. Mexicans might give you directions even if they don't know *where* the hell they're sending you, so as to avoid giving a direct, *"I don't know."*

Some cultures, like Filipinos and many Arabs, actually prefer to use English as the language of business, rather than stand by in horror as American executives butcher the local tongue. Deadlines and punctuality are regarded with suspicion in most non-Western cultures. And what we call nepotism, Latin Americans call common sense: hiring someone you can trust. Thursday is the day of rest in Egypt and Afghanistan; Friday is a day off in Somalia and Pakistan. Africans may step close to you, invading what you're used to as personal space; if you step back, they may feel rejected. The Chinese burp to indicate satisfaction. Asking a Saudi Arabian host about the health of his wife is considered impolite. Malaysian friends grasp both hands in greeting, while Venezuelans give a full embrace and a hearty slap on the back.

Read up on the local culture before you go, and save yourself some embarrassment or even hostility.

Foreign Currency

Go with travelers' checks. It's the best, safest, most convenient way of dealing with money in another country. Your ATM card may not work if your personal security code is more than four digits. Foreign ATMs also might not allow you to move cash around in your various accounts, so if you plan to use your card, make sure all the funds you need are in your checking account before you depart. Charge cards often have good rates of conversion to local currency, but be sure to exchange some cash for foreign currency at your local bank *before* you depart. It's best to hit the ground running; otherwise, you could be stuck getting ripped off at the airport money-changing kiosk. Once abroad, it's best to exchange your dollars at a bank—they give the best rates.

Remember to split up your money: Put some in a suitcase, some in your wallet or travel pouch—so if one or the other is stolen, you're not cleaned out.

chapter five

Digs: Finding a Place to Live

Renting

The difference between $400 a month and $600 a month, the difference between having a roommate or not, and the difference between having to pay for heat or having it included can be $2,000 or $3,000 over a single year. If you spend two solid weeks to find the perfect place, that can translate into $1,000 a week in savings.

Let's start with a simple question: What do you need? Not want, but *need*. For example, Todd *needs* two bathrooms. That's because when it comes to morning cleaning rituals, Todd's girlfriend clocks in at just under an hour and a half. (I suspect her routine includes lots of effort on her hair, which overflows with curl on weekdays but is arrow-straight on weekends.)

Other needs might include a garage (for those new wheels you buy in Chapter 7), a first-floor apartment (for the lazy), or a five-minute proximity from work (for a part-time firefighter). Keep this "Needs" list short.

Next, write down your *desires*. This list can be long and even indulgent. A vast lawn (for chipping golf balls) or a small lawn (less mowing)? Conveniently close to a supermarket, or safely out of reach, to avoid your late-night craving for a half

How the Real World Really Works

139

gallon of Rocky Road? A huge bedroom to fit your king-sized waterbed, or a little bitty one because you hate vacuuming? Do you want a dining room, a basement, a den? Perhaps you'd like to be within walking distance of a swimming pool. Maybe you want your *own* pool.

AGENTS

Except in New York City and a couple of other metropoli, most real estate agents don't bother with rentals. In New York, however, most of us try to find a pad without an agent—and fail. Dealing with agents is cutthroat and expensive—their fees are often two months' rent, which can mean anywhere from $1,500 to $3,000 or more. That's a whole different set of rules, which can include payoffs and shady dealings. Talk to a local.

When you do deal with an agent, don't tip him off on negotiations. Don't let on that your friend Lisa has given you exactly three days to find a place and get off her couch, or that you have $200 in the bank, or that you have $20,000 in the bank. Your agent is not your friend.

YOUR BASE CAMP

You start paying rent once you move to another city, even *before* you have an apartment. That's right. While you're searching, you're probably crashing on the couch or floor of a friend. Expect to spend $100 on this person. You should arrive bearing gifts—CDs are better than booze, because it's clear that the CD is for your friend alone. The next day he or she should come home from work and find fresh flowers or a new plant or a sparkling bathroom or a fridge chock-full of groceries. Never underestimate what a pain it is for your friend to have you staying there.

WHAT CAN YOU AFFORD?

You shouldn't saddle yourself with a rent of more than 35 to 40 percent of your gross income. That includes housing costs, like commissions, bribes, heating bills, phone bills, and so on. If your salary is $25,000 a year—which comes to $2,100 per month—your upper limit is about $800. Remember, that includes electricity, water, and all the rest.

SCOUTING APARTMENTS

If you can, quiz the tenants. Ask about landlords—how long do they take to fix things? What should you expect to pay for water, heat, electricity, "protection," and any other local expenses? Where do they park? Visit the house during both day and night. The sunlight brings out the little defects. Nighttime brings out the annoying traffic, loud neighbors, menacing passersby, and so on. You should look for:

1. **Bugs.** Open dark cabinets. Look for roach traps in the corners.

2. **Hot water.** Try the fraternity prank of flushing while the shower is running. Does it become scalding hot? Then you may have a problem, since the same thing might happen whenever the neighbors flush, too.

3. **Light.** Is there enough natural light? On the flip side, will the morning sun burst in on you, rousing you out of bed before you'd like?

4. **Electrical sockets and phone jacks.** Are there enough for your needs—your roommate's phone, your modem, and so on?

SHARING

If someone else has an apartment and you're looking to become his or her roommate, you'll likely end up chatting for fifteen minutes in the kitchen. Your potential roomie is sizing you up. Worry number one from his or her point of view: your stability and ability to pay rent. Worry number two: lifestyle questions—how loud is your music, do you spend all weekend lounging in front of the TV, is there a danger of your girlfriend or boyfriend becoming a constant presence? Worry number three: will you share the cleaning, the grocery shopping, and other chores? Whether you move into a new place together, or move into an established one, set ground rules from day one:

- **Food.** Do you want to share the grocery bill and shopping right down the middle? What if one of you travels a lot, or eats out, or eats a lot, or buys food the other doesn't eat? Will you share common foods, like milk, taking turns to buy them?
- **Newspapers and magazines.** Who will pay for the subscriptions if you both end up reading them?
- **Cleaning.** You need a schedule. Usually one roommate is neater than the other and ends up doing the dishes because he or she can't stand the pile. Don't allow yours to become an *Odd Couple* situation.
- **Property.** Can she borrow your tennis racket? Your car? Your VCR? Your computer? Your CDs? With or without permission?
- **Lights out.** At what time can you expect the stereo and TV to be turned off?
- **Boyfriend/girlfriend rules.** You can end up with a third roommate quicker than you can say "dinner and a movie." This can be a drag. Not only are you constantly reminded that *you* don't have a boyfriend or girlfriend, but you end up paying half the rent and getting a third of its value.
- **Watching TV.** How much TV do they watch? This ties up the living room and can be a distraction.

- **Phone time.** Some roommates I've known have had a big problem fighting over this. It might be wise to set loose, approximate time limits at the beginning of your roommateship. And look out for Internet junkies; they can tie up the line for hours.

See Chapter 8—Law—for information about negotiating your lease.

Buying

Buying a home is not a big deal. Nothing more is at stake than your preciously hoarded cash, your already shaky credit rating, and perhaps your freedom for the next ten years. After all, if you blow it—overpay, choose a lemon, whatever—it won't cost you more than $5,00 to $50,000, and possibly your spouse.

Start by reviewing the previous section on renting a home. Many of the same rules apply.

NEEDS

Again, ask yourself a simple question: What do you *need*? Second, make a list of your *desires*.

AGENTS

Now it's time to find a real estate agent, so here are a few words about them. They work strictly on commission: no fees. Generally, there are two agents—one represents you (the buyer), another represents the seller—each of whom takes somewhere around 3 or 4 percent of the final price. These are sometimes *negotiable*. You must ask about that; the agent will never volunteer.

WARNING: Any agent has his or her own "listings," and might push you toward them. For example, suppose Mickey

Realtor represents 1301 Pluto Place, 99 Minnie Mile, and 545 Goofy Street—that is, Mickey is the agent for those *sellers*. Then you come along, looking to *buy*. Even Homer Simpson could figure out which houses Mickey will want to show you first, even if they aren't the perfect match. Because if you buy 99 Minnie, Mickey gets *two* commissions, from both you and the seller.

Picking an agent is not so different from selecting a doctor. There's no secret: you ask for recommendations. Talk to a few agents, and choose one who sounds like she knows what she's talking about and isn't trying to rip you off. How many years has she been in the business? Does she have time for you? Will she condescend to deal with your measly price range? Can she show you properties listed by firms other than her own?

If all your friends hate the real estate agents they know and you can't get a recommendation, then go to a few *open houses*. Those are days when a house for sale is open for the public to poke around without an appointment. Chat with the agent. Do you feel comfortable?

Are you an impatient shopper? The type who muscles through the supermarket express lane even though you have 64 items? The type who buys the first pair of blue jeans you see at the mall, even if they're Toughskins? If that's you, listen up: Do *not* rush to pick an agent. Do your homework, talk to a bunch of agents, then make your move.

WHAT CAN YOU AFFORD?

Another way to ask this is: Have you ever played golf? If so, you probably recall a hole somewhere with a lake about 200 yards from the tee, a classic design that requires a tough decision. Do you play it safe, punch the tee shot 150 yards or so, and *then* hit over the water? Or do you pull out the driver, smash the ball the 260 yards that you were clearing on the practice tee, clear that pond, and earn high fives from all your friends?

If you're like most people, you pull out the driver and slice it into the drink. That's the reason that vulgar words are often heard on the links.

A mortgage is like that water-hazard hole. You might think you can afford $900 a month, while the bank decides that because you have only $5,000 in the bank and you still owe $15,000 in college loans, you can only afford $500 a month to play it safe. Here are two basic rules of thumb:

1. Your monthly payments should be no more than 28 percent of your gross income. That includes principal and interest on the house, homeowner's and mortgage insurance, and property taxes.

2. Your overall monthly debt—including the payments in rule 1, plus credit card bills, and college loans, gambling chits, car payments, and so on—should not exceed 36 percent of your gross monthly income.

Let's say your salary is $30,000 a year—which comes to $2,500 per month. Rule 1 suggests you can afford $700 a month for a house. But if you're already writing monthly checks of $200 to Chrysler, $130 to Penn State, and $70 to Circuit City, rule 2 dictates that you can't spend more than $500 a month for your house—even though you're on the same $30,000 a year salary.

LOCATION

Four factors affect price: condition, price, terms, and location. But some real estate agents say there are only three factors: location, location, location. Location can never be changed, so it's the most important. Do you want to be close to the office? Is access to public transportation important? Is the house or condo near parks, biking trails, swimming pools, tennis courts, grocery stores, drugstores? Is it within walking distance of a school? If you plan to have kids in the next ten years, what do you think of the school district? Is the area safe? You don't want to have to look over your shoulder at night. Do the cars whiz by at unsafe speeds? What's the neighborhood like at night? Is there any morning rush-hour commotion? Are there cranky old people who will call the cops if you play your stereo? Are the property tax rates okay? Is there a nuclear power plant nearby? A landfill? A plane route? Train tracks? Are lots of homes for sale? Is there a vacant lot across the street? Undeveloped land is a wild card; vacant lots can turn into strip malls or even strip clubs.

STEPS FOR SEARCHING

1. Get a list of "drive-bys" from your agent, as well as from your newspaper. Simply cruise by and look from the outside, decide if you like the house's appearance, the neighborhood, and so on.

2. As you drive around the neighborhoods, you'll see houses that are *For Sale By Owner,* or *FSBOs.* Your agent does not particularly want you to look at these homes—he won't show them to you because the owner isn't offering a commission. While you don't want to screw your agent over, you should definitely check out any FSBOs which intrigue you. Just call up and schedule a look-see.

3. Once you have a list of drive-bys you liked, call your agent and tell her which homes you'd like to see, how many you'd like to see in a single day, and other logistics. She will then arrange for you to see the homes.

4. Go on tour. This isn't Intro to Psychology—note-taking is vital! Be a pain. Try everything—faucets, sockets, toilets, gas stove, and air conditioning or heat; look under the cupboards; and look for leaks in the roofing or other structural problems. Remember the jury's tour of O.J.'s house? Jurors found a fire burning in the fireplace, fresh

flowers, and a cute bedside shot of O.J.'s mom. Don't fall for that, or for the smell of chocolate-chip cookies, or any of the other tricks people use to make their homes feel homier.

5. Once you've selected a house, you need to get a loan. This is complicated and boring and I don't want to get into it here. The basics: the bigger your down payment, the better your loan terms. Some down payments are as low as 5 percent, and can go up to 25 percent.

6. Get a home inspection. For a new home, ask for an *H.O.W. (Home Owner's Warranty)* from the builder. Sometimes the builder gives cheapo warranties that don't protect you from much, so be careful with them. Talk to other people who live in the development—just ring their doorbells and ask what they think of their humble abodes.

    If your home is not freshly built but is being sold by the owners, then for $200 or so you can get a home inspection. The inspector will check out the structural foundations and the like. You probably won't know a rotting I-beam unless it fell on you, so paying the money for a pro makes sense, if only for peace of mind. Some states require an inspection. But, once again, you need a reputable inspector, because their liability is not larger than *their fee*. So if you buy a $90,000 collapsible box that falls apart two days after you move in, you could sue the inspector only to recover your whopping $200 fee (that is, not for the $90,000 you just wasted). Unless, that is, your agreement included a guarantee.

7. Make an offer. An offer is a legal document. Your real estate agent writes the offer, which lists the price, the amount of the down payment, the amount of *earnest money* (the deposit), the date of closing, the date you'll take possession of the house, and how you plan to finance it. You can also detail anything else—that you require an inspection, that the refrigerator remain, and so on. Be spe-

cific. If you want a termite inspection, for example, the offer should include when the inspection will happen, who will pay, what will happen if the house fails inspection (probably that you reserve the right to withdraw the offer). An offer should include a deadline, maybe 24 hours for them to respond. You want to keep pressure on the sellers, so they'll fear losing a deal.

HOW MUCH SHOULD YOU OFFER?

How much below the asking price should you offer? That's a question you (and your agent) must research—how much did other houses in the neighborhood sell for? How long has your particular house been on the market? If it's been a while, the sellers might be willing to drop the price significantly. Similarly, if you've learned why the owners are moving out, you might know whether they need to unload in a hurry.

Most of the real estate books steer you wrong here. They advise against *lowballing*, or offering a price way below what's being asked. But these books are all written by real estate agents, so that's not surprising—here your agent has a different motivation than you do. She wants the sale *now*, and she doesn't gain by your savings (in fact, she loses). Let's say the seller is asking $100,000. The house has been on the market for two months, so you ask the agent what he thinks about offering $80,000, with the hope that you'll bargain and end up at $90,000. Your agent might say, "Forget it," "They'll be insulted," or "We can't really offer less than $90,000," with the idea that you'll end up settling at $95,000.

Well, for you the difference between ultimately paying $90,000 or paying $95,000 is a huge deal. For the agent, though, your $80,000 initial bid guarantees either an outright rejection or protracted negotiations. Either way, you might want to look at more houses, which means more work for him. He, of course, just wants to get the sale done and get on with his other customers. In fact, if you don't buy this house, then you may not find anything else you like and may decide to rent, or to switch agents. In other words, the agent has nothing to gain by a lowball offer. You have everything to gain. So *you* decide. In most states, the agent is legally obliged to make any offer you want, no matter how low.

EARNEST MONEY

When making an offer, you also give *earnest money*—$500 is common—to the real estate agent, who holds it in escrow. If your offer is accepted, the $500 goes toward your down payment. If your offer is refused, you get the money back. If you back out of the offer after it's accepted, you lose the earnest money, unless your offer makes specific exceptions (for example, if the house fails a structural inspection).

WHAT HAPPENS NEXT

The seller will accept your offer, reject it, or make a counteroffer. If you offer $80,000, the seller might counter by dropping the price from $100,000 to, say, $94,000. If you actually come to a deal, there's all this boring, incomprehensible legal jargon about your *title,* which establishes that you actually own the house. At this point, it's often worth buying *title insurance.* This protects you if, down the road, some creditor shows up with an agreement that states *he* owns your house—that is, that the past owner illegally sold you this house. This can be a sizable legal mess if you haven't had the title officially transferred into your name.

chapter six

Making Home Sweet

POSTDORM LIVING

Organizing Your Closet

Your closet is a disaster. Why? Because you treat your closet like a Thanksgiving dinner. You fill your plate again and again with turkey, stuffing, yams, rolls, gravy, potatoes—wonderful foods, but taken together over the course of time, they make you feel bloated and immobile. Only with great effort can you lift yourself up and plod to the couch, where you fall like a stone. That's why Thanksgiving TV specials are so incredibly stupid—their producers know you're so stuffed you can't even lift the remote to change the channel.

Part of the transition into adulthood means confronting your stuffed, bloated closet. There's so much dead wardrobe weight that needs to go. Those saggy, holey, "emergency" pairs of underwear. The "gardening" and "painting" clothes that you would otherwise never wear in public. The suit you'll wear once you lose those fifteen pounds. The stained white oxford and torn silk shirt, which, of course, won't mend themselves. The seven pairs of Nikes that lost their treads long ago, but they cost so much in the first place you can't bear to chuck them, so they become your "lawn-mowing shoes" (regardless of whether you actually have a lawn). And if you have an Imelda Marcos–esque shoe addiction, now is the time to confront it. Step one is admitting you have a problem. Step two through twelve are pulling out every pair of shoes that, no matter how good they looked in the store, just don't ever make it onto your feet. They've got to go.

Then there are the T-shirts. According to a recent poll, college graduates acquire an average of 27 T-shirts over the course of their four years, counting various purchases from the athletic department, fraternities, sororities, clubs, concerts, festivals, and fundraisers, and counting the cool ones they stole from their various roommates. This poll may be a tad unscientific—only three people were sampled—but it's probably true anyway.

Management consultants talk about the 80-20 rule, which says that 80 percent of most companies' revenues come from 20 percent of their customers. Your wardrobe is probably no different: Your favorite duds make up 20 percent of your wardrobe, but you wear them four out of every five days. So dumping many of the "occasional" clothes from your closet will only help you become more organized and ultimately find the things you really want to cover your body.

Don't try to kamikaze, all-at-once method on a bulging closet. Try one hour. Put the B-52s' *Roam* CD on your stereo to get you moving; when the final strains of "Follow Your Bliss" fade away, you're done with closet rehabilitation for the day.

Get a big Hefty trash bag and two empty boxes (ask at the liquor store for freebies), and make your bed. Your goal is to purge at least a third of what you touch. Take the clothes from your closet, one by one. Toss the garments that need major repairs into the trash bag—we both know you'll never get around to it—where you won't be able to see them, so you won't have the sudden desire to "rescue" them. The Salvation Army gets the nice but rarely worn sweaters, slacks, and knit shirts; just fold them into the boxes. Lay "keepers" on your bed.

After the hour has slipped away, act *fast*. Rehang what's on your bed. Give any wool clothes some space—they need breathing room. Don't hang sweaters; they'll droop. Move your jackets to the hall closet if there's room, or leave them on your bed. Go to the Salvation Army *now*, stopping only to lose the trash bag, or else some of your castaways will somehow escape from the box or bag and make it back into your closet. On your way home, glowing with the appreciation of the Salvation ministers (ho ho ho), pick up a couple of sturdy hooks from the hardware store. They're for those bulky jackets still lying on your bed; they take up too much space to be in your bedroom closet.

After you repeat this one-hour process a few times, spruce up your closet a little. Install a lamp, for starters. If there's no electrical outlet, you can find a cheap battery-op model at Woolworth's. Mount a bar on the back of your bedroom door, where you can hang everyday pants (otherwise, you'll toss them on a chair, where they'll fall off, and then you won't know whether they're in the clean pile or the dirty pile). Sure, you can sniff at them, but mounting a bar is easier in the long run.

Some people are into "space savers," so keep an eye out for shoe racks, belt hooks, and other organizers that you could live with. If your shelves are deeper than a foot, install a board twelve inches deep to limit the shelf space. That's right—*deduct* shelf space. When shelves are too deep, clothes get pushed into the netherworld at the back the closet, where they won't be seen for years, only to return faded and way out of style.

I've read wardrobe tips that only the most anal-retentive people could follow. "Organize a closet by color." "Have your color analyzed by a professional consultant." "Place a week's worth of jewelry in sandwich bags, then poke then through the hangers of your week's outfits." "Pre-tie scarves over hanging sweaters." If this sounds viable, you're uptight enough that you certainly don't need to read this chapter (although if you're that anal, you're probably reading it anyway).

For the rest of us, here's one simple rule to live by: Undress by the laundry basket, rather than using the walk-around-and-peel-off-clothes-at-your-leisure method. If they're clean enough to wear another time, hang them inside out so that next Thursday you don't have to try to remember whether you wore that shirt once before washing or four times.

Laundry

HERE ARE SIX EASY STAIN-PREVENTION TIPS:

1. Let your Chanel No. 5 or Mennon Speed Stick dry before you put on your blouse or shirt.

2. Keep your briefcase on a table, not the floor. Otherwise, it'll pick up dirt and then rub against your pants or skirt.

3. Buy silk shirts one size too big. That way, you'll minimize those gross underarm sweat stains.

4. When you get home from work, change into your casual clothes. It sounds like (and is) common sense, but the reality is that you arrive home exhausted, flick on the TV, order a pizza, and next think you know, your Brooks Brothers oxford is sporting a big spot of pepperoni grease. It doesn't have to be the ugly tan slacks that your father wears; jeans and T-shirts are fine.

5. Designate a super-comfy, extra-large, button-down shirt as your "work shirt," and give it a prominent hook so it's easily accessible. Wear the shirt for cooking and other messy projects.

6. Wear an undershirt, T-shirt, or camisole under your office clothes. It will absorb sweat, which enables you to hang up your business duds without washing them.

WASHING TIPS

1. My freshman-year roommate had a simple way to keep a supply of clean underwear: For the first five weeks of school, he bought about two dozen new pairs of boxers. While this didn't work over the long term, you should invest in a dozen extra pairs of socks and underwear. They're cheap and don't take up much room in the washing machine. The big advantage is that you can cut your laundry days down from once a week to twice a month.

2. Don't do the "scrounge for quarters" bit every Sunday. Stop by the bank on Friday, or hit the grocery store and get a $10 roll. That way you won't be tempted to shove three weeks' worth of laundry into a single machine.

3. Turn the clothes inside out before washing to minimize fading.

4. If you have your own washing machine, run an empty load of hot water and a large cup of distilled vinegar every once in a while. That cleans the hardened soap out of the hoses.

5. Button up buttons and zip up zippers to avoid tangling and wrinkling.

6. Don't change the sheets. Strip them, wash them, dry them, and put them right back on. That way you'll avoid the Herculean contortions of folding them.

7. Make sure you empty the lint filter before every load. Otherwise, it'll cost you a few more quarters to get the clothes dry. Also, use a lint brush, not lint tape. The tape leaves a residue, which, much to the delight of the companies that make lint tape, ultimately attracts *more* lint.

IRONING TIPS

1. It's a nightmare. Ironing wastes time, occasionally damages the clothes, and certainly weakens the fibers. So look for knits, corduroy slacks, and other no-iron fabrics. When shopping, crunch up the clothes. If they wrinkle, forget them and move on.

Vanity Notes

1. Soaps and shampoos are essentially all the same; they just have different perfumes and different ad campaigns.

2. Conditioners should not be used every time you wash your hair. Do not use your nails to work in the 'poo— just your fingertips.

3. When you shave, the longer you soak the whiskers in water, the better. Fill the sink with hot water, instead of running it constantly while you shave. Strive for long strokes. Many people do two runs: the first with the grain, the second against it to finish up the missed spots.

4. If you're buying cheap sunglasses, choose green or gray, as they're most likely to be properly UV protective.

5. Find dropped contact lenses by using the vacuum cleaner and a filter, like a sock.

6. Don't skimp on ties; stick with silk (note: real silk ties do not cost $3) and wool. Those polyester things look *really* bad.

7. If you fear a receding hairline, avoid baseball caps and long hair; while in the shower, massage your scalp at some length with conditioner. Baldness is primarily hereditary, but exacerbated by clogged follicles and poor circulation in the scalp.

2. Don't overload your washer and dryer; small loads reduce wrinkles. Other antiwrinkle actions include rinsing the clothes in cool water rather than hot (this also saves en-

ergy), shortening the spin cycle on the washing machine, and removing clothes from the dryer when they're still a bit damp. If your clothes are going to sit in the dryer for more than a few minutes after they're done, then don't set the heat to the highest setting. Otherwise, you'll be stuck with creases.

3. To erase wrinkles without ironing, mist the clothes with water, then throw them in the dryer on low heat, along with a damp towel and a fabric softener sheet. Or hang the clothes in your bathroom while you take your morning shower; if you're the long, hot shower type, the room will steam up enough to ease the crinkles.

4. As a last resort, iron. Spray the clothes with a bit of warm water. If you have distilled water (not Evian or any other mineral water), use that in your iron. Otherwise, pour distilled vinegar into your iron every once in a while, and let it dissipate through the steam holes to remove mineral buildup.

Books

If you haven't been through your book collection for a while, it's time to dig through it. First, group the titles you could donate to the library or sell to a used bookstore—will you *ever* look at the Russian economics text from your junior year? Yes, yes, you did a beautiful job highlighting it, but let it go. Next, pack up books you'd like to save but don't need to have conveniently accessible. You might want to save books from your childhood, for example, but won't need them handy. Label those boxes in BIG LETTERS on both the top and sides, so in two years when you want a particular title, you won't have to burrow through every single crate you own.

After the boxed books are out of the way, examine the remaining tomes. Is there enough room for them? Often, people fill their bookshelves, then pile up books on floors or tables, when they should simply ante up for more shelving. Bookcases aren't that expensive. If you're in a back-to-the-simple-life kind of mood, you can also build bookcases—yes, even you, who can't hammer a nail without smacking your thumb senseless. And if aesthetics aren't Priority One, stack plywood boards on bricks or concrete block, layer by layer, and voila—a bookshelf.

Do you loan out your books? After giving one out, skip ahead a month or two in your calendar and write, "Call Marlon about returning *The Godfather*," or else the loan is likely to become permanent.

Buying Stuff

APPLIANCES

Computers, VCRs, stereos, and CD-ROMs become obsolete so fast that there's no point in discussing any particular models in this book. Look to *Consumer Reports* for that kind of wisdom. But there are some common tips that apply no matter what machine you buy.

No matter what a store's return policy, contract law requires them to replace a defective product or give you a refund. Buy with your credit card when possible (just be sure to set aside the cash to pay it off, in full, right away). A credit card gives you two advantages: many of them, like American Express, double the manufacturer's warranty; also, according to federal law, if you're in a dispute with the merchant, you can just notify the credit card company and you won't have to pay the sum in question until your conflict is resolved.

Traps

Once again, beware "interest-free financing." This goes for all appliances. Let's say you accept a Crazy Mikey's Home Appliances in-store charge card, which charges no interest for ninety days. So you buy a $1,000 stereo on January 15. Since the purchase is "interest-free," you wait until April 20, then use your tax refund to pay Crazy Mikey. That's ninety-five days, so you'll owe a measly five days' worth of interest, right?

Probably not. The trick is that Crazy Mikey will probably charge you *back interest* from the date of purchase. So instead of five days' worth of interest—somewhere around three bucks—they'll demand $60! In other words, make sure you *never* go past the "interest-free" time limit.

Another big moneymaker for Crazy Mikey is extended warranties, beyond whatever the manufacturer offers. Mikey will have plenty: theft protection, "acts of God" insurance that covers things like lightning-based power surges, routine maintenance, parts-and-labor, blah blah blah. It's a bit of a paradox: Why are they pushing you to buy protection against an item they're telling you is high-quality in the first place?

As a general rule of thumb, you probably don't want these warranties. For starters, obtain a Visa or American Express card that doubles the manufacturer's warranty—that's free coverage. If you generally crave peace of mind, try to limit your warranty purchases to items new to the market—like the latest notebook computer. They're more likely to require repairs than items like tape decks that have been perfected over decades.

It's been around longer than Elizabeth Taylor: the bait-and-switch. Yes, you know what it is, but you still fall for it, especially with home electronics. For example, suppose they advertise a JoJo Brand 486 desktop for $799 and you come running, only to be confronted by a swarthy salesman who freezes you with techno mumbo jumbo:

HIM:
That JoJo 486 has a two-part duplicator on its video RAM card. You don't want that.

YOU:

I don't?

HIM:

Do you?

YOU:

Well, what does a duplicator do?

HIM:

[feigning shock at your ignorance] It maintains the data transfer at a continual rate. With a two-bit card, your graphic interface will not be able to handle any quadrant application.

YOU:

[embarrassed at your ignorance] I see.

HIM:

What you probably need is an IBM 986, like you see over here. It's got everything: CD-ROM, 4 gigabyte IDE hard drive, fourteen-four internal modem, power steering, antilock brakes—

YOU:

[interrupting] How much is that one?

HIM:

Just $99 a month, and with that you get $2,300 in free software, plus a lint-free cloth—

YOU:

$99 for how many months?

HIM:

Until you die, actually, but with our extended warranty. . . .

The solution is both simple and a pain in the neck: Do your homework, so you *know* which model you want. Read the computer magazines or consumer magazines and ask hacker/audiovisual junkie friends. Then, when you see your dream machine on sale, don't take any crap, like "we're out of stock." Play hardball. "This is a bait-and-switch scheme," you'll say in a loud voice. "How do you advertise a product when you don't have enough in stock? What kind of place is this? I have a legal right to get that machine, isn't that true?" You get the idea.

Some stores sell "factory-serviced" or "reconditioned" items. That can mean many things, but two things are sure: The item is not the spanking-new product off the Sony assembly line, and it's cheaper than the real McCoy. A "factory-serviced" computer might mean the Intel chip has been replaced with the less regarded Cyrix or that the Toshiba monitor has been replaced with a Samsung; it might even mean that the product is used. Usually, this invalidates the manufacturer's warranty.

Superstores are a good place to start for low prices, and even they often have room to negotiate. Experiment by offering to pay 5 percent less than the ticket price, and if they say no, insist that the offer be taken to the manager. If it's rejected, walk out. Sometimes they'll catch you on the way out, and if not, it's no sweat to come back tomorrow and pay full price. Also, January and February tend to be the best times to buy—after Christmas, when walk-in traffic is slow and most retailers are looking to unload their inventory.

Stick with brand names that you know. An experienced hacker will know that Seagate and AST are quality IBM clones, for example, but that Librex is not. You probably won't know the difference, so ask around before you buy. Compaq, Dell, Packard Bell, NEC, and Toshiba are all major brands with at least decent reputations in computers. Bose, Onkyo, Aiwa, and Denon are all solid stereo choices.

FURNITURE

There's no way around it: Furniture is expensive. Figure that whatever you buy for your first apartment will last until you get married, and take a bit of time in this—especially guys. A lot of guys I know think nothing of spending *months* searching for the perfect stereo but won't spend more than half an hour picking out a couch and a table for a cool $1,000. So don't just sit there! Here are a few tips:

1. Go to a decent store. Furniture stores are notorious for "Going out of Business" sales that turn out to be annual events, and other such deceptions; you want to buy from someone who has a reputation to protect.

2. Look for dark colors or patterns. Face it: you're a klutz. You'll spill Diet Pepsi on the sofa. You'll wipe salsa onto the futon—or at least your friend Andrew will. Avoid any fabric that needs to be dry cleaned, since it won't wear that well.

3. Be a minimalist. That's all I'll say about that.

4. Antiques can be a good buy, as can sturdy furniture from garage sales and people who are moving away. Push gently on whatever you're buying to see if it's stable; check to see if (all) the drawers glide or if you have to rip them open; examine any hinges or table leaves or braces on shelves.

5. If you're buying cabinets (this is an advanced purchase), look for a Kitchen Cabinet Manufacturers Association sticker (no joke). Make sure any drawers have ball bearings (they'll glide smoothly) and that the corners are grooved together rather than just glued.

When buying *anything* that costs more than $50 for your pad, save the receipt!

Eating at Home

GROCERY POOR

Food. Even if you're skinny, you'll blow a couple grand on grub this year. The average family spends more than $4,000. Up until now, your grocery store experience has had just two chapters. First, you rode in the cart, begging Mom to buy Sugar Smacks *and* Cap'n Crunch. (Don't you hate when non-Crunchers call it "*Captain* Crunch?") Then came phase two, where you walked directly from the beer section to the express checkout.

This section deals with phase three—groceries for grown-ups. I've always been a little skeptical of the traditional advice. The experts have all sorts of ideas that supposedly save you "thousands" off your annual food bill. Clip coupons. Buy the no-frills brands. Eat more meals at home.

Yeah, right. Who has time to spend clipping coupons for a lousy 20 cents off Raisin Bran? You always forget to bring them to the grocery store anyway. Of course, the no-frills brands suck, don't they? And is skipping restaurants such a savings? Sure, if you buy a quarter rotisserie chicken, baked potato, and Coke at the local KFC rather than cook the same stuff yourself, you'll spend $3 more. But the time it takes at home—defrosting the chicken, preheating the oven, adding spices, washing and putting away the dishes—adds up to around an hour. And you're worth more than $3 an hour, aren't you? (This is how I like to justify spending my limited resources on oh-so-delicious KFC.)

Still, whether you eat in once a week or for every meal, here's what you need to know about grocery shopping. For starters, never shop when you're hungry. You probably know this, but you do it anyway. I did a very nonscientific study to prove this point: One Sunday I went to a local A&P after dinner and my bill was $25.53; the next Sunday I shopped *before* dinner and spent $46.77. (True, I ended up with two extra cans of Pringles and a box of Oreos, which requires vanilla ice cream, as well as three frozen pizzas, which in turn necessitate a six-pack of Molson's to go with them.)

SUPERMARKET LAYOUT

Those stores are designed, naturally, to make you spend all your money. The one item you're most likely to drop in for—milk—is *always* in the back. Bread, too. Meanwhile, the owners want you to walk past their shiny, happy, colorful fruits and vegetables, their aromatic cookies, and everything else.

Then there's the shelving. All the big-markup, convenient items are on eye level, like lentil soup or cake frosting or Minute Rice in a bag. The dried beans, sugar, and generic long-grain rice—on which the grocery store makes a smaller profit—are next to the floor.

Beware the handsome displays at the end of the aisles. Conniving grocery store engineers often place products, like 8,000 boxes of chocolate-chip cookies, in configurations that make you think they're on sale. Often, they're *not*.

WAREHOUSE CLUBS

Yes, the savings *can* be terrific. But be cautious. My parents, who are really into this Sam's Club thing (almost as a sort of social outing), get carried away with the atmosphere, working themselves into a buying frenzy. They'll go with the intent to buy blank tapes for my little brother, and they'll leave with a gallon jug of oil (which doesn't fit into the fridge), a 50-pack of AAA batteries (they have no appliances that use them), and a 20-pound box of detergent (which Mom can't lift).

On the other hand, if you pack tuna for your lunch every day, the warehouse clubs will sell you 10,000 cans for just over fourteen cents total, so you *can* save a lot, if you avoid impulse buying.

BRANDS

The difference between Kellogg's Frosted Flakes and No-Frills Econo-Buy Sugared Flakes O'Corn is . . . nothing. Except for the fact that Kellogg's spends tens of millions of dollars every year pasting Tony the Tiger all over your television. Jeez, this stuff is just cornflakes and sugar. What could possibly go wrong in the recipe?

In fact, many no-frills products are *exactly* the same as their brand-name competitors—where the same factory processes green beans from a single farm, with some batches going into cans marked Green Giant and other batches poured into cans marked Food King Green Beans. In other words, no-frills doesn't necessarily mean no-quality. True, with some items the economy brands stink: paper towels come to mind. The only way to find out is to try them.

COUPONS

Coupons are overrated. Every once in a while your local TV news will do a glowing story on a coupon queen who regularly feeds her family of five for $2.54 a week, saving at least a hundred bucks. God bless her. What the reporter doesn't say, of course, is that it takes 20 hours a week to clip, file, cross-index, redeem proofs of purchase, and the like—which works out to $5 an hour in savings. So don't feel guilty if you throw away the glossy coupon section of your Sunday paper.

To use coupons sensibly, remember three things. First, you probably don't want most of these products, so a 20-cent coupon on a $3.00 frozen dinner you wouldn't otherwise buy is really a $2.80 loss. Second, a discount off a brand name is often still more expensive than the no-frills product; don't take 50 cents off $3.00 Ore-Ida french fries when Pathmark fries are $1.50 cheaper in the first place. Third, some products, like cereals, issue ton of coupons, so learn to wait to buy them until you've got the coupon.

In-store coupons often offer the biggest savings. *Member cards* are now becoming common, which automatically register sale items without your having to rip apart circulars for coupons. They also serve as check-cashing or check-writing cards. Finally, because the scanner enters your purchases into a database, the member card will allow grocers to mail you coupons for the items you buy most. It's a bit Orwellian, but quite convenient.

Watch out for the scanners. Their constant mistakes are well documented. They are *nine or ten times more likely to overcharge* than undercharge, usually because they miss the sale items. To keep an eye on this, when you transfer the groceries from your cart onto the belt, unload any sale items *last*. Then keep an eye on the cash register readout, and speak up before the seven-year-old cashier presses Total. Otherwise, the store manager has to come over with that stupid key to correct a mistake, which takes forever, and the people in line behind you get very cranky, and you get only 75 cents off anyway.

LABELS

A 1990 federal law declared that food labels must give more accurate information. Food corporation lobbyists, of course, got hold of Congress, and thousands of dollars in political contributions later (surprise), loopholes were born. Thus, food *ads* are still permitted to be wildly deceptive, even if the label is not. So trust the label, not the ad.

MORE TIPS

- Compare brands and package sizes by looking at unit prices—the price per ounce, for example—rather than the item price.

- Don't buy nonfood items, like shaving cream, at the grocery store. Stick with discount drugstores.
- Dig through the milk cartons to pick out one from the back—that's where you'll find the ones with the most distant freshness date.
- Farmers' markets offer local produce in season, and beat grocery stores on three counts: local produce is usually cheaper, fresher, and less likely to be treated with pesticides and waxes. Waxes and pesticides are very common, which is why you should wash and peel grocery-bought vegetables and fruits whenever possible. Strawberries, grapes, lettuce, and potatoes tend to contain the most pesticides. "Organic" is good if certified by your state or some organization; it means no pesticides were used to grow that food. But the word is often abused for marketing purposes.

Eating (and Drinking) at Home: Party Version

HOW TO THROW A DINNER PARTY

You already know how to throw every variation on a drinking party, right? The kegger, the mai-tai, the rum punch mixed in the bathtub, the "quarters" tournaments—that's old news. But one of your favorite postcollege discoveries will be the dinner party. It's very grown-up and everyone will be *so* impressed with you that you'll want to throw one every few months. In addition, you'll get to see a bunch of your friends in a single night, which will ease your expensive calendar of social obligations. The idea is to have from six to twelve people over; picking your partners, of course, is just as important as picking the menu. Try for an even distribution—a few old friends, a few colleagues from work, someone you know from the gym, and so on. If you invite six people from work and two old friends, you'll have a problem—everyone will gossip about the office and those two poor souls will be left in the cold.

Your job as host or hostess is to keep the conversation in areas of general interest: why Richard Dreyfuss is so annoying, the last *Seinfeld* episode, whether Sting has a Jesus complex, the photo exhibit that just opened at the local museum. Politics can be a fun topic, but dangerous, especially the Middle East and Rush Limbaugh. Try to avoid recounting old war stories where half the dinner party has no idea what you're talking about. Sex is *always* an excellent topic, especially after a few bottles of wine. But save it for dessert time, otherwise you'll never talk about anything else.

Every guest should bring one item: beer or wine (it's up to you to specify red or white), lentil salad, pecan pie, fresh strawberries, bread, Brie and crackers, a tablecloth, whatever. Couples count as a single guest, although if they offer to bring two things, take them up on it. Write down what everyone is bringing; otherwise you'll forget and end up with six loaves of bread and no beer. (When you're the guest, you might also bring a nondinner gift—a CD, flowers, the latest Tom Clancy paperback. That way you're sure to be invited back. The nicest gesture, however, is to *insist* on washing the dishes. This is pure class.)

The menu, of course, can be as simple or elaborate as you like—from lasagna to *coq au vin*—but try for dishes that don't need a lot of attention as your guests arrive. For example, if you want to serve chicken, let it bake in the oven with some fresh herbs rather than try to stir-fry it while greeting your friends. Steer clear of foods that must be cooked for a precise amount of time, like fish, which dries out quickly. If you tell people to show up at 7:00, expect to put food on the table between 7:45 and 8:15. As they arrive, take any coats (and gifts), then usher them toward your couch—don't let them crowd around the kitchen. If they're as nice as you are, they'll offer to help; don't give them make-work tasks, but if they want to set the table, let them have at it.

HOW TO THROW A WINE-TASTING PARTY

All of our college weekends were the same: We got wasted. But now you're a grown-up. Maturity is expected. Therefore, society has invented a way to get wasted in style: the wine-tasting party.

It's pretty straightforward and a lot of fun. Invite, say, five people over to your pad—plus you makes six (twelve people is probably the party maximum, since a single bottle will serve only so many tasters). Each brings a bottle of wine matching your instructions. For example, you might order "red wine from South America, priced between $10 and $20." That way you won't be comparing apples with oranges, or with grapes, or, um, well, you know what I mean. Have bread, cheese, and fruit for snacking between glasses, and to make sure you don't get drunk right away.

Now the idea, in pure terms, is to line up six glasses in front of each person. This presents a problem. Few of us have 36 wine glasses. You have two choices: use plastic (reasonable, but kind of tacky) or ask everyone to bring their own glasses. You could even make do with a total of eighteen glasses by drinking the first three bottles of wine, then rinsing out the glasses and sampling the final three bottles.

You can taste them "blind" (put the bottles in paper bags, just like the hobos do), but this isn't such a great idea if you're not all wine aficionados, since the point of a blind test is to guess the wine—what grape, what country or region, what year, even what vineyard. In any case, the basic idea is that you all drink the same wine at the same time, then sit back and make clever comments about color, weight, "nose" (the type of aroma and its power), body, balance, clarity, and "finish." Since most of us couldn't tell a 1985 Cabernet Sauvignon from a 1997 Manishevitz Concord Grape, it's always smart to invite one person who actually knows what the hell he or she is talking about. That's how you learn.

Etiquette

Yes, deferential behavior toward women is still generally expected.

- Men are supposed to walk on the curb side of the street, even with two women (not in the middle, even if it makes him feel like a big man).
- Men should usually open doors. But they should go first through revolving doors or ones that open inward.
- At a restaurant, a man might offer to carry a woman's drink from the bar to the table.
- A man shouldn't offer his hand to a woman to shake. She should offer her hand first.

Whenever shaking hands, take off any gloves you have on. And stand up if you're sitting.

To introduce two people when you've forgotten one of their names, try using titles such as "This is my personal trainer". With any luck, the unnamed person will pick up the slack. Give both the first and last names when you know them. Also, *don't* repeat names in reverse like in the movies. ("Clark Gable, I'd like you to meet Vivien Leigh; Miss Leigh, Mr. Gable.") It's cheesey.

If you have the car keys, it's nice to unlock and open your passenger's door before your own. Similarly, if you're the passenger, reach over and unlock the driver's door, as in the movie *A Bronx Tale*.

At a Restaurant

When the food comes, don't use the salt and pepper until you've actually tasted the food to see if it needs any. Deciphering the utensils is easy: work from the outside in; that is, start with the fork farthest from you. Put the fork in your left hand to cut your food, then switch it to your right hand to eat. The spoon is not a little cup; eat the soup, don't drink it. The knife can be used to cut a salad (this used to be a *faux pas*). Your fingers are okay for finger foods; you needn't use a fork for carrot sticks, not even at Buckingham Palace.

Elbows can go on the table after everyone is done eating. Do not, however, push your plate away to make room for your elbows. Don't put dirty silverware on the tablecloth. When leaving the restaurant, leave your napkin on the chair, not on the table. At a dinner party, don't ask for seconds; wait to see if they're offered.

At the Theater

If you're late, wait in the back until the usher seats you during a scene change. When seated, stand up to let people past you in your row. Plays, musicals, and operas are not like the movies—don't talk and don't eat. Keep hard candies to a minimum (the unwrapping noise is annoying). And don't take pictures, especially with a flash, which can be dangerous for the actors.

On the Telephone

- Don't leave your TV on while calling—it's so obvious when it's wailing in the background, making your caller worry that your attention is elsewhere. Likewise, the radio should be low.
- If you're disconnected, the initial caller should do the calling back, unless you accidentally pulled the plug or something, in which case *you* should call back.
- Call-waiting interruptions shouldn't last more than fifteen seconds. Start your conversation with someone who "beeps in" by announcing that you're on the other line.
- Watch out for speakerphones and conference-call features. Suppose Marc comes into your office and asks if you and

Jane want to join him for dinner. You call Jane on your speakerphone: "Want to come to dinner with me and Marc?" "Let's just you and me go," she replies. "Marc's been getting on my nerves." Everybody loses in this situation. So don't put someone on speaker without advising him or her in your opening line.

- Cellular and car phones are expensive, so don't ask to borrow them with impunity. Your friends or associate may not care if the company picks up the tab, but if she's spending her own money, she's less than excited about subsidizing your social life.

  In any case, limit your use of your own cell phone as well. The technology improves every year, but it's still common (and annoying) to lose a caller for 20 seconds who is driving through a tunnel or past an antenna. Also, don't chatter aimlessly while sitting in public places—it's disturbing to those around you.

- Get to the point of your call within 30 seconds.
- To get off the phone, try the phrase, "Before we hang up . . ."
- As several physicists have noted, writing implements and pads often escape into thin air. Try attaching a pen with a cord to your phone. It's a bit tacky, sure, but worth it.
- When leaving a message, avoid playing telephone tag by giving a precise window of time when you're available. Instead of "I'll be in all afternoon," say, "I'll be free from 2:00 to 3:00."
- As voice mail has become increasingly popular, we can now leave detailed messages. Do so. If several facts must be communicated, hang up, write down the complete message to make sure you nail every point without meandering, then call back and leave the message.
- It's okay to call when you expect someone *not* to be there, so you can leave a message. The other person is busy, too, and will usually appreciate the convenience. (This tactic is unacceptable for dumping your girlfriend or boyfriend.)

- "Hello, I love you, won't you tell me your name?" Yes we like the Doors as much as Oliver Stone does. But while the answering machine message is often confused with a road-trip mix, it is *not*. I personally support the death penalty for people who leave long musical intros on their answering machines.

- Be careful about screening calls. This leaves people suspicious, every time you *don't* pick up, that you are actually there but don't want to speak. In turn, this leads to awkward messages like, "Hello, Denise? Are you there? Hello? Pick up if you're home . . . Hello? I guess you're not . . ." In the end, your friends will stop leaving messages and will carry a lot of inner resentment instead.

chapter seven

Wheels

I grew up surrounded by guys who knew cars. They didn't just change the oil, they didn't just detail the hood, they could entirely rebuild cars. I had other skills. Sure, I could quote every Woody Allen movie, line for line. But my car skills were limited to three words: "fill 'er up." This chapter is for people like me who don't know a V-6 from a six-pack.

Picking a Car

What exactly are you looking for? Basic transportation for weekends? Something that will hold you for a 75-minute daily commute? A babe magnet? Little cars are cheaper, easier to park, and get better gas mileage. Big cars, of course, are big. They're also generally safer. Read some of the car magazines, like *Car and Driver*. Ask your friends and family; test-drive their cars.

Once you have a basic idea of what you want—a small, four-door sedan, for example—find out what each manufacturer offers as a "small car" model. There's Chevrolet Cavalier, Acura Integra, Dodge Neon, Eagle Summit, Ford Aspire and Escort, Geo Prizm and Metro, Honda Civic, Mazda Protege, Mercury Tracer, Nissan Sentra, Saturn, and many more. That's a lot to choose from. To make it even more confusing, each model offers various *trim lines*—LX, DX, SE, GT, and so on—

whose differences can include handling, engine size, and "standard" option packages. So if you find ten small car models, the trim lines effectively multiply your choices to 40.

Considering Options

On top of picking a model and trim line, you've got options to consider. Air bags, antilock brakes, rear window defroster and wiper, four-wheel drive, traction control, air conditioning, and a central locking system are all good choices. And don't forget the CD player.

Some options that should give pause:

Power windows	They're expensive to replace.
Larger engine	Unless you're towing a boat, most base engines are fine.
Cruise control	Your mind wanders.
Cellular phone	Calls are so damn expensive!
Adjustable ride control	This is a gimmick—skip it.

Upholstery preservatives, rustproofing, and extended service contracts are all dealer tactics to bump up the final price. But you can protect the upholstery yourself by buying the product yourself for a couple of bucks; the rust is probably covered in your manufacturer's warranty; and the extended warranty is useful only for unreliable cars, which you're going to avoid anyway. Right?

Considering Price

To further narrow the range of cars, you've got to think about price. A Geo Metro might go for $9,000, while an Acura Integra is about double that. Don't ask the salesperson to recommend a car. He's looking to unload his hard-to-move models.

Taking a Test Drive

What is a test drive? Half an hour of experiencing what the car feels like, trying to park it, accelerating at lights, trying a sudden stop on a back road, parking it in your driveway, changing the radio, trying the wipers, and so on. Ask yourself:

- Is the driving position comfortable?
- Do the controls work easily and logically?
- Are the seat belts easy to buckle?
- Is it comfy in back? Sit there for a while.

After the drive is over, get out of the car. Thank the salesperson. Get her business card. Go home.

Learning the Lingo

Bump: When the sales guy tries to push a more expensive model (or set of options) on you. Also when he tries to raise the price right before you sign.

Dealer invoice: What the dealer paid the carmaker.

Destination charge: Shipping costs, which the dealer passes along to you. The dealer typically doesn't inflate those costs, so they aren't usually negotiable.

Factory-to-customer rebate: You know those ads that announce that you can "get $1,000 CASH BACK!"? You can use this money toward a down payment.

Factory-to-dealer rebate: Sometimes the carmaker—Ford, Honda, whoever—builds too many of one type of model. Rather than have 5,000 Escorts or Accords sitting outside a factory, they give rebates to the dealers to get rid of them. Whether the dealer passes some or part of the savings along to you, well, that's another question. If you know about the rebate, naturally, you can use it during negotiations.

Trim lines: See the section on "Picking a Car."

Options packages: Many carmakers bundle options together: power steering, power brakes, air conditioning, power windows, and ejection seat might make up Option package A. It costs less than if you bought each item separately, but the package may have items you don't really need—like the ejection seat.

Abbreviations:
  wagon = station wagon
  auto = automatic transmission
  RDR = retail delivery report (the dealer's end-of-month report)
  AC = air conditioning
  cassette = AM/FM radio with cassette player
  cruise = cruise control

Doing Your Homework

You need to find out what the dealer paid for the car you're considering. Then you want to offer him a profit of a few hundred bucks. Many bookstores and magazines, most notably *Consumer Reports*, offer up-to-date guides that list factory invoice prices. Add in the cost of the options you want, and you know what the dealer paid for the car.

Consumer Reports is one of the best-known price guides. You can call them at 800-933-5555. Name the model and the options you're considering, and they'll tell you roughly what that car would cost a dealer. Then they'll fax you a Price Report that includes any rebates offered by the manufacturer. In 1996, this report cost $12. Kelley's Blue Book also provides this service. Call 900-Blue-Book or hit their Website at www.kbb.com.

The Salesperson's Side of This

From the salesperson's point of view, you are a liar. You lie about your trade-in's condition, what other brands you're considering, what you're willing to pay, and what other dealerships you've visited.

He'll give you the regular treatment—the firm handshake, the buddy-buddy eye contact, the big smile—all while sizing you up. Are you a tire kicker (a customer who talks as if he or she knows a lot about cars, but doesn't)? A "lay-down" (someone who'll be an easy mark for full price)? A "roach" (a person with lousy credit)? A "be-back" (a customer who promises to return and doesn't)? This process is called "qualifying." He'll chat, asking you about your family and where you work, in order to figure out whether you're window shopping or not and how nice a car you can afford.

A salesperson wants to sit you in a car, any car. New cars have a nice smell, a tight feel, and the customer's emotions help the salesperson do her job. If you sound uncertain about your needs, the salesperson will usher you over to another model and start singing its praises. She's trying to unload a slow-moving car on you, because there's probably some extra commission involved. Look at the door jamb for the date of manufacture. If the car is more than a few months old, the dealer is dying to get it off the lot—he pays interest on the car until he sells it.

Every day, the salesperson hears, "Give me the best price on this car." If he answers directly, he won't stay in the business very long. He has to make you go through the bargaining process, so he'll counter with, "I really don't know what they're going to sell this for, but I want to get you the best price possible." Every day, someone quotes him the factory invoice from *Consumer Reports* or another buying guide, and he has to bluff: "This model is a top seller, all across the country. The boss is not going to go much below sticker because the past dozen or so of these Toyotas have been sold within a week or so of arriving."

He'll bother you for a deposit—$100, whatever—take your offer to the manager, and leave you with a brag book—all the positive reviews and awards from the various car mags. The back-and-forth starts then, and if he feels you slipping away, he'll call in for backup—a veteran closer who could sell sand on Palm Beach.

When to Buy

In most cases, the odds are stacked in the salesperson's favor. He's done this a thousand times before. He's got a quota and is willing to be pushy. He can selectively give you information and present everything in a light that suits him. Just as you wouldn't trust the spokesperson of Merck Pharmaceuticals if there were a sudden recall of one their drugs, you can't expect to trust a car salesperson. She's a publicist, not an objective mediator.

Go to buy the car when times are slow. The end of any month is a good time—most customers don't have as much disposable cash, and the salespeople's quotas are looming. Wintertime is always good, especially after Christmas, when nobody has any money.

You should never go to a dealership to negotiate if you don't have several hours to kill. Taking an afternoon off from work for the final negotiation could save you a few hundred bucks. Early afternoon, around 2 P.M., is good: the lunchtime lookers have gone back to work and the lot is probably empty. You can sit there patiently, making the salesperson take very small incremental offers to the manager. They usually stall for a while between offers to try to wear you down—which won't work if you brought a book or magazine to pass the time.

The Negotiation

Your goal, of course, is to pay as close as possible to what the dealer paid the factory. If he paid $15,000 for a new Bronco, your ideal is to pay him $15,001. Meanwhile, he's hoping to have you fork over $18,000. The price you agree on will fall somewhere in between those two extremes. The average gross profit is 6.5 percent. On a $15,000 factory invoice, that's $975 profit. From that profit, the dealer must pay the salesperson, the rent, and all other overhead.

Now pay attention. Dealer cost, or *factory invoice*, does not reflect *holdback*. *After* the dealer sells you that new white

Bronco, Ford headquarters sends him the holdback—a check for 2 or 3 percent of the sticker as a bonus. In other words, you don't want to pay 6.5 percent over factory invoice. You want to pay a "spread" of 3.5 percent over the invoice—around $15,550 total. That means the dealer got $550 from you. To make up the rest of the $975, Ford sends him $425.

Sometimes two sister companies make the same car with different nameplates: the Plymouth Neon is the same as the Dodge Neon, and the Ford Taurus is just like the Mercury Sable. You can use this to your advantage by comparing prices at different dealerships.

HERE'S WHAT TO EXPECT

- "Get any of the competitor's quotes—I'll beat them." Don't take the bait. Insist that you want a firm price quote, or you won't do business with that dealer.
- "How much would you pay?" This is a trap. Just repeat that you want a quote from him, which you will compare against the other dealers.
- "How much do you think I should make?" Same thing. See the preceding trap.
- "Your information is wrong; we paid more for that car." Ask to see the factory invoice. If she's bluffing, she won't show it to you; if not, then you'll learn the correct cost of the car.

After you get through that you want a quote, he'll go talk to the sales manager, leaving you alone and hoping that you'll get anxious. He'll return and offer a price—perhaps accompanied by "That price is good only until 5 P.M. today" or some similar tactic. Thank him for the quote, tell him you're going to other dealerships, and leave.

OTHER DEALERS

Once you've got your first price, get on the horn. Call a few different dealerships and repeat the preceding process. Or, if you're feeling particularly ambitious, you can try for an "insider's" price. Follow these steps.

First, call and get the manager's name. "I'm writing a note to the sales manager working Honda, and I wonder if you could spell his name for me." Get it. Hang up. If you ask the sales manager, you'll just get a sales rep, who doesn't have the authority to do this kind of dealing.

Then, call back later: "This is Mike Goldstein for Charles Barkley, please." Since these guys deal on a firm-handshake, first-names-only pseudofriendly basis, your next step is:

"Hi, Charles. This is Mike Goldstein. I need a black Honda Prelude SI with auto, AC, bags, and cassette. Do you have one in your inventory?" You should peruse the lot the day before, so you know what's there. This way, you come across as someone who knows exactly what he or she wants, and is ready to buy today.

Barkley might respond with:

a. "Yes. How much you want to pay?"

b. "I do have a *teal* SI, with stick, and a bunch of others ones."

c. "Are you in the business?"

Your replies to these responses are:

a. This is a trick question. Again, never name a total dollar amount. Just say what you'd be willing to pay over the dealer invoice. And don't ask. Tell, with confidence. "Seven over." Period. Shut up. In other words, you'll pay him $700 more than what he paid for it. No matter what the options package, you're offering him a profit of $700.

- If he takes the offer, you offered too much.
- He'll probably try to bump you. If it's more than, say, $200, then either he's not giving you much of a deal, or your initial offer was way out of line. No matter what, say "That's too strong." Again, confidence.
- If you do get a good price, repeat your name and say "Sounds good. I'll call you by the end of the day." If you can't get a better deal elsewhere, call back soon and close the deal.

b. If only one or two of the options on the model he's trying to sell you are different from what you ideally want, you might decide to pursue this car. If not, however, ask him when he could get a car with exactly the options you want.

c. "No, but I can take immediate delivery if we agree on a price." Then go back to the first step to negotiate price.

Closing the Deal

Once you have a firm quote that you've comparison-shopped to death, close the deal. Ask the salesperson if there are any advertising fees or "conveyance" fees (paperwork costs). *Then* get a price on your trade-in—you have to research what your old car is worth so you can negotiate effectively. (*Consumer Reports* will give you that information if you call 900-446-0500, $1.75/minute) The salesperson will then try to push warranties, rustproofing, paint sealant, and other extras. Don't take them. Don't, don't, don't.

Finally, you have to arrange financing. You should go to a bank or two before your car negotiation, just to see what rate is offered. The dealer can usually offer a better rate than the bank.

Whatever you do, take your time in reviewing the sales papers. Tell the salesperson it'll take you 20 minutes to read through them so she won't stand there reading over your shoulder. The language in car contracts is (not surprisingly) very dense, but you want to go slowly to make sure the numbers you verbally agreed to are the same ones written on the contract.

Buying Services

If buying a car seems too intimidating, try a *buying service*. You call (find them in the Yellow Pages under "Automotive Purchasing Consultants") and tell a rep what make, model, color, and options you want. Their buyers—ex-managers of dealerships—call local dealers, get the best quotes they can, then pass them on to you. If you want to accept one of them, the club calls back the dealer, who then prepares the paperwork. You basically go and sign.

The average fee for one of these services is about $140. Buying services can be especially worthwhile for women and minorities, since statistics show that these groups, when negotiating for themselves, pay significantly more for cars (242 percent according to a Harvard Law School study) than white men. Evidently, the sales staffs are quicker to give price breaks to white men.

No-Haggle Dealerships

This is a new trend: dealers who have one-price, no-haggle policies. Saturn, for example, sells its cars exclusively this way—whatever you see on the sticker, that's the price. Period. Though you'll save stress, they're not necessarily better deals. Depending on exactly what you're looking for, and your threshold for (often) painful negotiation, this is an option that a lot of people are choosing and one that you should consider.

smoke means a worn engine. Check the taillights and brake lights, as well as the directional signals. Also, make sure to try reverse gear.

Shuddering, vibrating, or squealing during braking can be trouble. They might mean the brake pads are down to bare metal, which is costly to repair. Try a panic stop to see what happens—but warn whoever is in the car with you before you jam on the brakes.

While stopped, turn the wheel all the way from one side to the other. Listen for hissing, squealing, or groaning. Look in the rearview mirror for colored smoke; sniff for a burnt odor.

Put a drop of hot engine oil (from the dipstick) onto the exhaust manifold. If it sizzles like water on a frying pan, bail on the car. This means you need a new head gasket at best, and you have a cracked engine block at worst. Both are very expensive repairs.

Look for service stickers on the door, the radiator, on the air filter cover. When was the last inspection or repair visit? Snoop in the glove compartment for any records.

When you're ready to buy a used car, take it for an independent diagnostic check. You might pay $75 or so, but it's worth it to find out if the car needs $500 in repairs. Make sure the inspector knows the vehicle isn't yours, so he or she doesn't do the usual make-up-things-that-are-wrong bit. Call first and ask what the charge is for a complete diagnostic exam. Only after a car has passed your inspection do you negotiate with the seller.

THE NEGOTIATION

1. Start by saying, "What's your asking price?" Language is important—"asking" sends a not-so-subtle signal that you intend to drive the price down. Counter by letting them know that you're in such-and-such a price range. If their asking price is *way* below book price (the number you looked up at the bank), you may want to move quickly.

Otherwise, after telling them what range you're in, explain that you will get back to them "after I talk with the other owners on my list."

2. Let several days go by. If the car is sold, offer congratulations and ask what it was sold for. If not, again query on the "asking price."

3. Make another call. Tell the seller that you are financially prepared to make a quick transaction for "the right car." "I'm reasonably interested if your car is in mechanically sound condition." At this point, let them tell you anything that's wrong, and assume they're minimizing the problem.

   Ask, "What is your bottom-line price for a quick cash sale?" If their price has dropped, repeat the amount, then set up an appointment to see it in daylight. If they offer the same price as before, then leave your number, wish them luck, and ask them to call if and when they are ready to sell for "a reasonably fair price" or "market price."

4. Show up to examine the car. Start your chat by repeating the amount they quoted in step 3. Write down a brief description of the car (including mileage) and the price you discussed (for example, "You quoted $3,000") on a piece of paper. Hand them the paper to get them involved in the sale. Don't talk about the price until everything else is clear, including the mechanic's check.

5. Examine the car as described in the previous instructions, and take the car for a test drive.

6. If you still want it, tell the seller you'd like a mechanic to give the car a once-over, but at same time ask the seller if he or she will accept a cashier's check as full payment. Again, don't bring up price. Don't have the seller come with you to see the mechanic. Certainly don't take it to someone the seller has recommended (he or she might suggest so-and-so because "he's someone who has serviced the car and is familiar with it").

7. Ask the mechanic to give a written report—and prices for all projected repairs. Ask which repairs are essential and which ones can wait.

8. Assuming that the car is okayed, make your offer with a cashier's check, made out in your name, not the seller's. You can always raise your offer by adding cash or a personal check, but the cashier's check helps make your offer firm. Tell the seller:

   a. "I've been looking at another car that's cheaper than yours." Give some details to indicate that the cars are comparable, like how the rival car has lower mileage but "yours looks nicer." Say "I can buy *their* car today for this amount"—wave your check in the air—"but since I prefer yours, I'll buy yours right now for the same price. Have we got a deal?"

   b. Or you could show him or her your mechanic's estimate. "Do you want to make these repairs, and I'll have it checked again afterward and buy for the price we originally discussed? Or I could make the repairs and we could deduct the estimated costs from the price right now. I have this cashier's check right here [for the quoted price less your estimate for the repairs]."

If they ask for a price from you, reserve it and say, "What's your rock-bottom price for the car as it is right now, if I take care of the $450 [or whatever] this mechanic estimated in repairs?" If they come down slightly, say politely that you're sorry, but it's still too much. Perhaps at this point you could split the difference.

Keep the conversation to a minimum after the sale—don't give the seller a reason to change his or her mind. You must get clear title to the vehicle (proof that the seller owns the car he or she is selling to you). If the seller still owes payments on the car, call his or her lender before you negotiate and inquire what the lender's requirements are for you to receive title and transfer. Make sure you won't have to pay any fee. Register the title with the state DMV. You might need to have the seller's signature notarized on a title transfer form.

chapter eight

Legal Headaches

Housing Problems

Steve "Flounder" Smith just graduated from SMU, having learned how to measure Bolivian GNP as a share of its foreign debt, how to integrate $5(\sin x - 1/2)\,\pi$, and how to shotgun a warm Old Milwaukee in just under four seconds. He's found a job in Houston (having read chapter one) and now needs an apartment, preferably a two-bedroom so he can find a room-mate and save money. Flounder learns that Pablo Matisse, a fellow alum from the Mustangs' class of '96, needs a Houston pad, too. They join forces.

After four days of searching in the 105-degree August sun, the duo finds an apartment. After duly investigating the neighborhood's safety (drive-by shootings are on the decline) and looking for bugs (only a small, single-parent cockroach family), they talk price. Mujibar, the landlord, asks for $1,000 including utilities. Flounder offers $900. Mujibar says, "That's the price, take it or leave it." Flounder and Pablo take it.

Mujibar presents them with a lease. It's a printed document, awash in legalese, so after making sure that the period is for one year and says $1,000 a month, they each sign it. Muji now wants a $3,000 security deposit. "The last tenants ripped me off," he explains. "They trashed the place and left in the middle of the night. You seem like nice kids, but I have to be careful." Pablo protests, but ultimately the two guys decide they don't want to keep up a housing search, and this way their last three months are paid in advance. They agree to move in on September 1, after Muji has the place painted. He also promises to fix the leaky toilet, the holes in the plaster where paintings had been hung, and the heater once he has the chance (as it's summertime, there's no rush).

Naturally, when September 1 arrives, the place hasn't been painted. Muji explains that the painter got tied up and the apartment will be ready on September 6 for sure. Pablo shacks up with some girl he met at the Morrissey concert. Flounder is forced to crash at the Red Roof Inn.

True to his word, Muji presents them with keys on September 6. One bedroom is a little bigger than the other. They flip for it; Flounder wins. Pablo is grumpy for three days.

Over the next four months, Flounder realizes that he loathes his roommate. Pablo smokes. He burps constantly. He *never* cleans up his dishes. He gets an ugly Eurotrash haircut. He hogs the phone. In October, he was late with his half of the rent, and Muji tacked on a $40 late fee.

Flounder finally confronts him. Pablo has beefs of his own: "My room is 20 percent smaller than yours, so I should pay less rent. It should be, like, a 60–40 split, dude. Also, if that Bruce Springsteen poster in the living room doesn't come down, I may have to kill myself. Or at least torch the poster."

Pablo decides to move out instead.

HOW THE LAW APPLIES

Here's how the vaunted American legal system applies to Flounder.

First, when Flounder was confronted with the printed lease, he was already at a huge disadvantage: Muji bought that form at a stationery store, most likely, and it was written by a lawyer for the real estate industry. Naturally, the terms are skewed in the landlord's favor. True, Flounder didn't have much leverage: He needed to find a place. Still, he should have examined the lease.

What to look for? For starters, does the lease specify when the rent is due, and what penalty will be imposed if it is not paid on time? Does it say who must make repairs or whether the tenant can make improvements, like adding carpet? Does it specify when the security deposit will be returned—and with or without interest? (Some states require the landlord to pay, say, 5 percent, which would be a not-so-shabby $150 in this case.)

When Muji said that gas and water were included in the rent, Flounder should have made sure it was contained in the lease. If not, he could have handwritten it; nothing fancy, just "Gas and water costs are included in the rental price of $1,000 a month." Also, even if their $900 offer was rejected, Flounder and Pablo should have tried a second time, maybe $970. As piddling as it seems to haggle over $30 a month, that ten seconds of being pushy could save you $360 over the year. Remember, every time Muji has to show the apartment, it costs him valuable time. He wants to get a deal done, too.

Another Flounder mistake: Giving a security deposit on a nonpristine apartment, without writing out exactly what was currently wrong with the place. You should make sure the landlord signs a list of defects, if any, and when they'll be fixed. That way, at the end of the year, she can't charge you for what she calls "your" damage when you can prove it was already there.

If defects aren't fixed, send the landlord a letter stating that unless the problems are remedied by such-and-such date, you'll pay to have them fixed and deduct the fees from the rent. You do not actually have the legal right to do this, but it often lights a little fire under the butts of lazy landlords. If that fails, unfortunately, your only remedy is to sue or vacate. If you vacate—that is, bail—under these conditions, you are not liable for any more rent. (Document the damage carefully, with photos if possible! Otherwise the landlord will fix it, then sue you.) You're also entitled to your security deposit, although in the real world, good luck getting it back. Most likely you'd have to sue for that, too.

The landlord's delay in having the apartment ready, from September 1 to September 6, was not unreasonable, but Flounder was entitled to some money nonetheless. His five days at the Red Roof Inn came to $175; he also shelled out $100 to store his belongings. This should be immediately deducted from the rent. September's rent of $1,000 should also be cut by one-sixth (that is, 5 days out of 30), which comes to about $165. Flounder should have spelled this out immediately upon learning of the delay, and asked Muji to sign a letter saying his hotel and storage expenses would be deducted. Otherwise, Muji might try to take the $440 from the security deposit a year later. Note that Flounder did not stay at the superlush Plaza Hotel—he's entitled only to "reasonable" expenses.

If a delay in moving in is long—maybe the landlord can't get the old tenant out—then, in some states, you might sue for breach of lease. Not only will you get your deposits back, but you can sue for damages. For example, if the apartment you end up with costs $100 more per month than Muji's, you can sue him for the additional $100 per month for the length of the lease. So for a one-year lease, the original landlord would owe you $1,200.

THE PABLO PROBLEMO

When Pablo bailed on the apartment, Flounder was *jointly and severally* liable for the *entire* rent. That means each of the tenants was individually responsible for the whole $1,000 per month. In other words, Flounder was screwed.

Flounder could have asked for a clause in the original lease making him liable only for his share of the rent, but Muji (and most landlords) probably wouldn't have agreed. In addition, Flounder was ripped off on the telephone bill: Since it was in his name, he owed the money, even though Pablo made those international and 900-number calls. (Note: Sometimes the phone company will waive 900-number charges that you claim weren't yours, since they're very sensitive to the fact that they make huge amounts by selling porn. They basically tell you, "Don't let it happen again.")

The Pablo situation is not uncommon, even among friends, let alone strangers. Flounder should have drawn up a straightforward contract with Pablo. Though it's not as awkward as asking for a prenuptial agreement, most people still feel reluctant to write it down. Believe me, a few minutes invested in a one-page letter will pay big dividends later. Oral deals have a way of undergoing revisionist history. The agreement should include what portion of the rent each person will pay, cleaning arrangements, whether groceries or utilities will be split evenly, who gets the one-car garage, what hours TV or loud music will be restricted, and so on. Even though you feel stupid writing this down when you just want to say, "We'll work situations out as they arise," the written agreement will be worth it—equal sets of expectations are created. Suppose Pablo thinks cranking his stereo until 3 A.M. is reasonable; Flounder thinks midnight should be the cutoff. This way, they hash it out up front—maybe they decide on 1 A.M.—and a clear line is drawn.

PRIVACY

You have a legal right to *quiet enjoyment* of your apartment, whether it is stated in your lease or not. That means that if the neighbors (in the building) are too loud, your landlord is responsible for quieting them down. The practical reality is that your landlord may respond to your protests by saying something like "Eat me." Naturally, the hassle of a lawsuit isn't worth it. But you might grab a practical legal guide from the library (Melvin Belli's *Everybody's Guide to the Law* is a good bet) and show your landlord the quiet enjoyment clause.

Can your landlord barge into your apartment? No. In most states, the landlord may enter your apartment to inspect for damage or make repairs, but must give you at least a day's notice unless it's an emergency.

RAISING THE RENT

Can the landlord raise the rent? If you have a one-year lease, your rent cannot be raised for that year. That's the essence of your contract. If the building is sold to another landlord, the new one, cannot raise your rent for the duration of the contract, in most cases. She'd have to be able to prove that she didn't know you lived there—which would be almost impossible to show unless you were out of town for six months *and* the previous landlord lied to her. You're 100 percent legally protected, though, if you *record* your lease at the county mortgage office when you first sign it, but you probably don't need to make this effort.

SECURITY DEPOSITS

Flounder should have made sure the security deposit was itemized. For example, he might have asked Muji to hand-write that the $3,000 would be broken down as follows: $2,000 to cover the last two months of rent; $800 as security against damages; $100 as a key deposit; and $100 for cleaning costs. Moreover, many states limit the total deposit to two months' rent—$2,000 for everything in this case. Still, in the real world, Flounder may have to pay an unfairly high deposit if he wants the apartment. Yet since he did, he gained leverage for any further disputes.

If your lease does not specify that the security deposit includes the last month's rent, you do not have the legal right to insist that the landlord use the deposit as the last month's rent. Unfortunately, that means he'll have a lot of leverage when you leave, because, as they say, possession is nine-tenths of the law, and he'll be holding that deposit.

Before returning the key, move your furniture and clean your apartment thoroughly, and try to meet with the landlord a couple of days before your lease is up. That way, if she sees problems, you can fix them yourself and save some dough. Ask her to write a check a couple of days in advance, so she can hand it to you on the spot. Take pictures of the clean, empty space as well, just in case; judges like photos. And insist that she meet you on the day that you're leaving, to talk about the apartment's condition face-to-face.

SUBLETS

Generally, a *sublet* is when you rent out an extra room, or when you rent out the whole apartment for a few months. An *assignment* is when you transfer the entire lease to another person, say, if your employer moves you to a branch in another city and you rent out your apartment for whatever time remains on your lease. Unless the lease specifically prohibits sublets or assignments without written permission, it's okay. If assignments are prohibited, but there is no mention of subletting, then the latter is okay. Some states and some leases now provide that the landlord must allow a reasonable sublet or assignment.

Flounder sublet his room to a guy named Noah. When Flounder did so, he became a landlord while remaining a tenant. He still owed the rent to Muji; he was owed money by Noah. He should have bought a standard sublet contract at a stationery store; that document would probably have a provision that gave Flounder the right to retake possession of the apartment if Noah failed to pay the rent.

The smart thing to do if you're leaving an apartment before the lease expires is to stay away from an assignment, if possible, and ask the landlord to release you from your lease and to sign up the new tenant. You do *not* want to be in the landlord business. If he refuses, ask the landlord if the sublettor can pay him directly, even though it's understood that you remain liable for the rent.

If you can't find another tenant and the landlord won't let you out of the lease, you can *surrender* it (move out in the middle of the night). The legal question is whether the landlord *accepts* your white flag. She can tell you this directly, but usually actions speak louder: Does she try to relet the apartment? (Some states require a *good-faith effort*.) If so, you're off the hook (except for any damage that exceeds the security deposit). If not, many states make her send you a letter explicitly stating that she's not releasing you from any obligations—and if she doesn't send the letter, you're off the hook.

JUMPING SHIP

If you abandon the place, the landlord can't sue you immediately for all missed rent. For example, if Pablo and Flounder had vacated their $1,000-a-month pad four months before the lease expired, Muji could not have sued right away for $4,000—unless there was an *acceleration* clause, which basically states that if you miss one payment, the entire balance becomes due immediately. Without an acceleration clause, the landlord must either wait until the four months are up, or file one lawsuit per month.

If you're a little behind in the rent, the landlord *cannot* change the locks and evict you. *Forcible entry* isn't allowed in almost any state, so the landlord has to notify you first in writing (such as, "Pay up in three days or get out"), then file an eviction proceeding. Perhaps two weeks after you are served with such a notice, there's a hearing. The judge may let you pay up then and keep the apartment. Or, if the judge accepts your excuse for not paying, you may stay without paying. For example, you may try to prove that the apartment is "unlivable," which might consist of two letters from friends stating that your heater doesn't work, copies of the letters you sent to your landlord telling him about it, and a photo of you in your apartment all bundled up (which, of course, doesn't prove anything, but they say a picture is worth . . .).

Another example of a valid excuse might be a canceled check you wrote to a repair worker toward needed work that the landlord refused to do on a timely basis. (You can't claim fees for your own labor, however.) Even if the judge rules against you, the landlord *still* can't physically evict you; the cops must do it.

Finally, there's the question of lawyer fees. Your landlord probably has a decent attorney; you probably can't afford one. The solution is often legal service organizations, like the Legal Aid Society (you have to be poor to qualify) or the local law school. The state bar association has referral lists, which still serve you better than the Yellow Pages. Go to a lawyer while the problem is in its early stages. Not surprisingly, landlords take calls from lawyers more seriously than calls from you.

Money Problems

There are two ways you can fall behind on loan payments: (*a*) you might lose your job, or (*b*) you might be a moron with no self-control, buying everything in sight. Avoid both scenarios. However, if you do fall behind on payments, the bill may be turned over to a collection agency. These can be annoying, so it's important to understand your rights.

According to federal law, a debt collector cannot contact you at inconvenient times, harass you, threaten to call the police, threaten to contact your boss, embarrass you in front of your friends, or tell you he or she is an attorney or government employee. In addition, many states don't allow him or her to contact you at work without your permission. Note that the creditor—the person you actually owe the money—is not covered by this federal law. Still, most states protect you from the creditor in much the same way.

Typically, a creditor *sells* a debt to a collection agency. If you owe $700 to Circuit City, they might sell the debt to the Godfather Collection Agency for $400. Now Godfather has the right to that $700. Perhaps Sonny calls, and you explain that the stereo was defective, that you returned it, and that you stopped payment on the check. Sonny explains that the matter is between you and Circuit City, but now he owns the debt and will sue if he doesn't get the money— and that after paying him, you should try to get Circuit City to pay you. This is illegal; tell him so. Here's how to stop Godfather:

1. Write them. Explain you won't pay, or can't pay, and tell them to desist with all contact. They must obey, except to tell you of further action (like a lawsuit).

2. Hire an attorney. Nobody messes with lawyers, and the added bonus is that not only Godfather but also Circuit City must deal *only* with your lawyer once you've notified them.

If you do get sued, however, *don't ignore it*. If you do, the creditor automatically wins and can tap into your bank accounts and garnish your wages (as in the movie *Fletch*). If you are disputing the sum owed, either hire a lawyer or gather documentation proving your point. Let's say you bought a used car, then find out the odometer was turned back and try to return it. The manager of the Lemon Lot won't accept the car, so you stop payments. Lemon sues you. Gather the appropriate evidence, including a letter from a mechanic verifying the tampering, your receipts, copies of letters you sent to Lemon, and state your case to the judge.

RENEGOTIATING LOANS

In cases, however, where you don't have enough money to pay your creditors, you've got to toughen up and deal with this crisis. Perhaps you lost your job. You have a car payment of $250 a month, college loan payments of $150 a month, and a minimum credit card payment of $100 a month, along with rent, utilities, and other necessities.

Step one is to figure out what you can afford of that $500 a month. Step two is to contact the three creditors, make sure you speak to the person who can approve repayment plans (rather than just a clerk), and honestly explain the predicament. If you can afford $200 a month, offer them 50 percent and add that each creditor will be offered the same cut. Ask them to waive late fees and penalties. You might offer to return to full payments once you find a new job. Or offer to send them a copy of your budget, so they'll be assured that you're not living extravagantly at their expense. A good-faith effort is often rewarded, and not necessarily out of any kindness: Merchants know that if they use a collection agency, it'll cost them anyway.

If one or two creditors go for your plan, go to the holdout(s) and mention that "NationsBank agreed to cut my Visa payments in half and waive all late fees—will you?" If they continue to refuse, explain that if this voluntary repayment plan doesn't work out, you'll be forced to file for bankruptcy.

BANKRUPTCY

Bankruptcy does not have the stigma of the old days, but it still destroys your credit rating, which could cost you tens of thousands when you buy a home. You'll need a lawyer to file for Chapter 7 or Chapter 13. You need a steady income for Chapter 13. A court-appointed trustee reviews your repayment plan, usually over three years, and often reduces the amount of debt. The $15,000 you owe, for example, might be cut to $11,000.

Under Chapter 13, most of your debts are canceled in Chapter 7. (There are exceptions. For example, if you throw a huge bash for your buddies the day before filing, you're still liable.) Ultimately, your assets are sold (though many are exempt, like your house and car) and the money is distributed to your creditors. You get a fresh start.

TRAFFIC TICKETS

It's your word against the police officer's. Guess who wins? Even with the Rodney-King-era distrust of the cops, traffic court has a judge and no jury. So when you swear you had the cruise control set at 55 and the cop says he clocked you at 70, or when you insist that you stopped but the officer claims it was a "rolling stop," you basically have no chance. Guilty. Case closed. Pay up.

Oh, you say you have a witness? That can change things. But if your witness is your boyfriend who was sitting next to you at the time, the judge isn't likely to be impressed.

Don't bother with an unprovable excuse, even if it's true. Even if the meter still had time showing when you returned, a judge has no reason to believe you. But if you were stopped for speeding on the way to watch your baby being delivered—and you have the hospital record in your hand—you might well soften up the black robe on the bench. If you didn't see the speed limit sign, go back and look for it. Maybe it's defaced, or knocked down, or covered by a branch. Photograph it from a few angles. Judges love hard evidence. It makes them feel like Ito, instead of having to pay the usual he-said/she-said guessing game.

Another tactic: Contest the ticket in the hope that the cop won't appear. It happens often enough. The prosecution may ask for a continuance; oppose that. Say, "I've gone to the trouble of fighting this precisely because the ticket was wrong, my boss gave me a hard time about skipping work, and ask that you dismiss the charge immediately."

You can also call the DA's office and find out which assistant handles the traffic cases. Plead your case. Perhaps you can get a mechanic to certify that your speedometer was off by eight, nine, ten mph. The prosecutors often make a deal—perhaps lowering your 90 mph ticket to a 75 mph one, which can save you money and, in the eyes of the insurance company, prevent your record from becoming soiled.

If your ticket requires that you appear in court, dress professionally. Why do you think O.J. rotated a dozen $2,000 suits during his trial?

Consider a lawyer. Call one and explain your defense. The reality is that she probably knows the assistant DA and can probably bargain your offense down, maybe drop your fine from, say, $300 to $100. She may charge $400 for his efforts, of course. But her fee may make sense if she prevents you from getting insurance "points," which cause your rates to shoot through the roof.

Just like on *Matlock*, the judge asks if you want to plead "guilty" or "not guilty"—she may also offer the chance to plead "guilty with an explanation." It's the same as "guilty" in legal terms, but the judge might forgive you if she accepts your logic. Or, even before asking about your guilt, she might offer the option of traffic school. The upside is that once you finish the six-hour class—which is incredibly boring; nobody pays any attention—the ticket is wiped from the slate. Insurance companies are kept in the dark.

If you plead "not guilty," how do you win? Be calm and methodical. Don't show any frustration toward the cops or the judge. Practice your statement a few times at home, but don't expect to read a statement—the judge probably won't let you.

First, the officer will testify against you. Then you may cross-examine him. Do not take an adversarial tone. If you are contending that he ticketed the wrong car, for example, your Q&A might go something like this:

YOU:
What time did you clock the speeding car?

COP:
Five-fifteen P.M.

YOU:
Rush hour?

COP:
Yes.

YOU:
Was traffic heavy?

COP:
Medium.

YOU:
When you first clocked the speeding car, could you see whether the driver was a man or a woman?

COP:
I was looking at the car.

YOU:
Could you see whether there was a passenger at that time?

COP:
No.

YOU:
Did you notice the color of the car at that time?

COP:
Yes. Black.

YOU:
Did you notice the license plate at that time?

COP:
No.

YOU:
Did you notice any bumper stickers?

COP:
Not at that time.

YOU:
Any dents?

COP:
No.

YOU:
Did you look away from the speeding car so you could safely get onto the road?

COP:
For a few seconds, sure.

YOU:
How long after you clocked the car did you pull me over?

COP:
About 30 seconds.

YOU:
Did you put your siren on right away?

COP:
Not until I sighted you.

YOU:
Was I speeding at that point?

COP:
No.

YOU:
When you pulled me over, did you pull in behind me?

COP:
Yes.

YOU:
Do you remember what the back of my car looks like?

COP:
No.

YOU:
This is a picture of my car. Could I show you this picture to see if it jogs your memory?

COP:
Yeah, that's right. I remember the "Meat is murder, but yummy" bumper sticker.

YOU:
You remember the dent, too.

COP:
Sure.

YOU:
Were you at all surprised when you saw the dent, after not having noticed it when you first clocked the speeder?

COP:
Not really.

YOU:
So when you first saw the speeding car, it went by in kind of a blur?

COP:
I saw it.

YOU:
Did you notice a radar-detection device in my car?

COP:
No.

YOU:
How typical is that in people who get tickets for 90 mph and above?

Maybe half have one.

At this point, you actually get to say, "I have no more questions, Your Honor." Then give your side of the story. You were coming home from work on your regular route at your regular speed. You saw a similar car zip by. You didn't see the driver, but you noticed the passenger because he was extremely attractive with a blond ponytail, singing along to "Jumpin' Jack Flash," which was cranking. You've never even gotten a speeding ticket, so it's certainly unlikely that you regularly drive 90 mph but have always evaded a citation.

Will you win? Probably not. In your favor: You speak well, dress well, are respectful, offer a reasonable excuse, have a photo, and went through the trouble of contesting the ticket. But even if the judge rules you guilty, she may give you a softer sentence or reduce the fine.

GETTING HURT

If you or your property is injured—you're zooming along on your mountain bike when someone runs a stop sign and smacks you—you can get compensated. This is called a *tort* (French for "wrong"). A *crime* is when the community (as in "the People versus") seeks justice; a *tort* is when you seek justice. Some wrongs are both crimes and torts simultaneously, like assault, where you and the district attorney can pursue separate cases against the villain.

You can sue for a host of wrongs—auto accidents, nuisance, medical malpractice, defective products. Don't try to handle this stuff yourself—lawyers not only win more (12 percent more, according to one study), but even after their fees you'll typically end up with more cash. Sometimes the damage is accidental, sometimes it's done on purpose. The law treats these differently.

ACCIDENTAL HARM

Accidents are the most common tort; in legalese, that's *negligence*. If you slip on a wet floor in a McDonald's, if you rent a bike with bad brakes and crash into a tree, if your barber nips your ear during your trim, you might sue for negligence. You have to prove not only that the event happened, but that reasonable care was not taken. Most cases come down to what constitutes "reasonable." If someone knocks his Coke onto the floor of Pizza Hut and you wipe out five seconds later, it would be hard to show that the waitstaff or busser had a *reasonable* chance to mop up, if they even had time to notice it.

Sometimes the event speaks for itself: If a Pizza Hut oven has a gas leak and explodes, they're going to be liable, even if the Hut can prove they took every reasonable precaution, such as having the oven inspected every month.

Pizza Hut might also argue *contributory negligence,* such as the fact that your shoelaces were untied. In some states, if you were partly at fault, you can't recover *any* damages. In other states, any damages would be reduced by the percentage that you were negligent. Obviously, that's quite an arbitrary number. If your shoes were untied, were you 25 percent negligent or 75 percent negligent? That's a jury decision.

Pizza Hut might further argue that you *assumed the risk.* Maybe a busboy went to get a mop but said, "Watch out for the spill," and you walked on it anyway. Another example: You're pitching in a softball game and the batter hits a line drive right into your face. That's part of the game. If the batter gets ticked off, though, and rushes the mound and pegs you with his bat, well, that's intentional, and assumption of risk does not apply.

You can sue only for the current value of property that's destroyed—not what it cost originally, not what it will cost to replace it. If your five-year-old Ford Escort GT gets totaled by a drunk driver, you could sue only for the $2,000 it's worth now, not the $10,000 it cost five years ago, not the $15,000 a new Escort would cost today.

Releases—written statements that tell you the defendant is not liable if such-and-such occurs—are not always valid. Fine print or indecipherable language, for example, may invalidate a release. The back of your ticket at Super Adventure King Amusement Farm might state that "by purchasing this ticket, Buyer releases Farm from any liability," but if the roller coaster falls off the rails and your leg must be amputated, they're probably not off the hook.

INTENTIONAL HARM

Let's say you get socked in the nose. Maybe José was joking around and meant to fake you out, but accidentally connected with your schnoz; or maybe someone told José that you called his sister a slut and he meant to break your face. The law sees a difference here: For injury inflicted on purpose, you can sue not only for *actual* damages, but also for *punitive* damages. Even if José actually meant to hit your friend Fed, who ducked, and connected with you, the *intent* transfers to you, so you can go for punitive damages.

Let's say you see your friend Christopher jogging down the street, oblivious, his Walkman blasting. You sneak up behind him and give him a friendly tackle and a proper noogie. You let him up and realize that it's not Chris at all, but a complete stranger. Can he sue you for intentional harm? Yes. Mistaken identity does not protect you here.

Most people think of assault as a physical attack, but that's battery—assault is the threat, and you can sue someone for assault even if he's kind of wimpy and you weren't really too worried about how much his punch would hurt. Battery includes not only your body, but your hat, your purse, anything you're wearing or holding close enough that it should count as an extension of your body. And battery includes more than just violence—an unwanted kiss is battery, unless it's from your Aunt Edna.

Let's say you're at Houlihan's and some annoying Indiana Pacers fan is cheering for Reggie Miller. This disturbs you. You order him to shut his fat mouth and make some choice comments about his mother (you've had a few beers), but to no effect—he's still mouthing off about Reggie. Finally, you ask him if he'd like to step outside to settle things like a man. He does. You break his jaw. Is that battery? In some states yes, in others no. Can he smack you for talking trash about his mom? No. Verbal provocation is rarely a legally acceptable excuse.

THEFT

Your leather jacket is stolen. Two weeks later, you see someone wearing it. You confront her. She says she bought it at the Salvation Army. Whose is it? Yours, even if she got it the way she told you. Can you grab the jacket off her shoulders? No, even if she's really small and you could whup her butt. (If someone stole the jacket two minutes ago and you are in hot pursuit, then yes, you can grab it back.) You'll have to alert the police, who will impound the jacket. Then you'll have to prove to a judge that the jacket was originally yours.

Finding a Lawyer

You don't need a lawyer if not much is at stake. For small claims or traffic court, you can get by without one. But for anything more serious, you'll have to open your wallet. Even lawyers don't represent themselves ("He who represents himself has a fool for a client," goes the old law school saying.) If it's a criminal case, you need to worry not just about jail time, but about a black mark on your "permanent record." (Yes, it sounds like school, except this might actually prevent you from landing a job.)

If you do need a lawyer, don't wait. The sooner he or she is on the case, the lower your chances of digging yourself a deeper hole than you're already in. Sometimes your opponent's lawyer will go after you quickly, trying to pressure you to sign a document before you have a lawyer to advise you.

For example, in a car accident where you were hurt but it wasn't your fault, the negligent driver's lawyer might tell you: "This is the best deal you're gonna get. If you hire an attorney that's your right, but it'll only cost you hundreds of dollars and he or she won't be able to get anything more than I'm offering right now. So why give away your money? Here, sign on the dotted line." Don't sign.

Whom to hire? Tough question. Recommendations are always the best place to start. Above all, you want someone with experience with your type of problem. You wouldn't hire Matlock to handle a divorce. But even a recommended lawyer who doesn't deal with your type of problem can probably recommend a colleague. Then there's your company's lawyer (assuming this dispute doesn't involve your employer), your union's lawyer, Legal Aid, even the local law schools, and the local bar association.

If you don't have any good leads and must start from scratch, ask yourself this question: How high are the stakes? For a dispute over a first-time DWI, it's probably okay to hire a young lawyer and save some money. For a murder case, you want to hire Johnnie Cochran if you can afford him, or the next best thing, even if it means wiping out all your savings and persuading Mom and Dad to mortgage their home.

YOUR FIRST MEETING

When you meet for a consultation (usually fifteen minutes or so, and often free), try to find out: Does she explain things in plain English? How much experience does she have with your type of case? (Experience in criminal law, for example, isn't specific enough—a lawyer who typically represents car thieves won't be your best bet if you're accused of systematically looting the office-supply fund.) Does she return calls?

While you're sizing her up, she's deciding how strong a case you have. Be honest. You're protected by attorney-client privilege, even if she doesn't end up as your lawyer. That means she's forbidden to tell anyone about your guilt or innocence, even if you confess to her. (There are very few exceptions: if you talk about a future crime, if you sue your attorney for malpractice, and so on.) So don't hide the weak sides of your case from your lawyer.

Larger firms tend to cost more, but might have more specialists with experience in your type of problem. Small firms are often better for routine matters, like DWI, because they give you more attention. Ignore the referral services in the Yellow Pages. They're just advertising for attorneys who need the business, and you'd do just as well by hanging pages of phone numbers on your wall and throwing a dart at them. Again, call the state bar association.

FEES

Lawyers' fees can be flat, hourly, or contingent. They are rarely negotiable. Fee disputes are the biggest reason for client dissatisfaction. Here's how to protect yourself. First, get the terms in writing, and take a day to read them and ask questions before giving your lawyer the go-ahead to pursue your case. This sounds like common sense, but if things are bad enough that you're seeing a lawyer, you're going to be very eager to sign one on. Expect to pay a *retainer* (down payment), then $100 or more per hour. Or, for personal injuries, a percentage of any winnings, ranging from 25 to 40 percent. A third is standard.

In addition, there are costs beyond lawyer labor: filing fees, travel, expert consultation, and so on. Even on a contingent fee, you owe these expenses, so make sure they're spelled out in advance. Look to see whether these expenses are deducted from the total award, or from your share of it. Say you win a jury award of $15,000:

- If Robert Shapiro gets his third of the winnings *first* (leaving you with $10,000), and *then* subtracts expenses, (say $3,000), you end up with $7,000.
- If Robert Shapiro *first* deducts his expenses from the $15,000 (leaving $12,000), and *then* takes his cut, you'll end up with $8,000.

So make sure your agreement states from whose share the expenses are deducted.

chapter nine

Surviving

BASIC SAFETY

Surprise! You've consumed $20,000 to $100,000 worth of education, and only now do you realize that your regression analysis of the whooping crane's talon strength won't help you protect yourself on the street. Your comfort with iambic pentameter isn't going to keep you from getting your butt kicked, or worse.

Okay, safety first, as they say.

Doors

Besides the fact that Jim Morrison is not *really* alive in South America, here's what you need to know about them.

You've always been told, "Don't open the door for strangers." Duh. Everyone knows that. So why do so many criminals get unsuspecting victims to unlock the doors for them? The point is, when they are scamming you, they sound *very* persuasive. The criminal might be wearing a uniform (police officer, plumber, and so on) or might know some bit of information that seems to put him or her on the up-and-up (like the landlord's name, or yours). Anytime you get an unexpected visit from what seems to be a professional, pull a Ronald Reagan: Trust, but verify. Whether it's the cops or a repair worker, keep the door locked and tell them you're calling the home office. Then do it. Ask if they can confirm that so-and-so was sent to such-and-such a place. Of course, don't call any number that the stranger offers. Use the phone book.

Here are some other door safety tips:

- Look for doors at least one-and-a-half inches thick, of solid wood (not plywood) or with a metal overlay.
- Medeco is generally considered the best brand of locks.
- You want at least one deadbolt lock.
- Sliding doors can be forced easily, so they need a bar on the bottom to wedge the door closed.
- A door's frame has to be sturdy. Don't put a $100 lock on a $25 door.
- A peephole is better than a chain, since reasonably strong men can force chains open, which means they promote a false sense of security.

Half of all assaults against women occur in their own homes— 80 percent of which are by unarmed assailants.

Travel Safety

When you travel, don't let the mail or newspapers pile up. Ask a neighbor to do the honors. Or have the mail carrier hold your letters at the post office, and call the newspaper office and have them hold your subscriptions while you're gone. Buy one of those gizmos that automatically turns your lights on and off at predetermined hours. Lights give the sense that you're home.

Don't leave your car parked at the airport, and don't dawdle on the way to pick up your bags; many thieves wait for bags to go around twice before stealing them.

Around town, lock your car doors, of course, even for a quick dash into the drugstore. Inexpensive car antitheft devices like The Club (which costs around $50) are deterrents only;

they are not fail-safe. A thief with a hacksaw can cut through the steering wheel in 30 seconds and remove the still-locked club. LoJack is an electronic tracking system that allows you to trace the car's signal and recover it. These systems are reportedly effective, but tend to run $600 or more.

Common Cons

- Every day I watch three-card monte dealers on the streets of New York, fleecing sucker after sucker. It's a version of the shell game—based on the premise that the hand is quicker than the eye. Some of the people who seem to be players are actually pawns working for the dealer. After the dealer lets you win a hand or two, these fake "players" will pressure you to up your gamble—"C'mon, c'mon, you already won"—and in the end your wallet will be lighter.

- For some reason, men love giant stereo speakers. Maybe it's Freudian, I don't know. In any case, young con artists will drive around a parking lot, grab you out of the blue, and say, "They miscounted at the factory and gave us an extra two pairs of speakers to deliver. How about a hundred bucks for these $1,000 speakers?" You open the box and they really are speakers, and hey, it's a *great* deal. Okay, maybe they are stolen property, but that just makes the deal seem even better. Then you get home, unpack the box, and there they are—bricks and styrofoam. What happened? They switched boxes on you. Or they sold you very attractive speaker shells without any woofers or tweeters inside.

- Someone—usually a little old lady or someone dressed in an impeccable suit—asks to borrow your cash card. "Could you just open the glass on this ATM? It's not reading mine." You figure why not, since you're not typing in your secret code. Of course, if you stopped to really think about it, you'd realize that *your* card won't let Granny access *her* account. But in the heat of the moment, you think you're doing a good deed; meanwhile, she watches you enter your own code, which she will type into the ATM once you've swiped your own card.

Carjackings

The simplest precautions—locked doors, never rolling windows more than a quarter of the way, keeping an eye on the rearview mirror, never leaving the keys in the car—will prevent you from becoming a Page One story.

On the road, there are two scripts for carjacking ploys. One is the "bump-and-rob," where someone "accidentally" hits your rear bumper. The other is "the Good Samaritan," where a driver pulls close to you and says or motions that you've got a flat or a leak. If you fall for either and get out of the car, the carjacker will rob you, then take your car.

A third ploy is police impersonation. Anyone can put a flashing light in his car, pull you over, and say he's an undercover officer. If this happens, drive slowly until you reach a well-lit area or streetlight and pull over there. Then roll your window down only a little and ask to see his credentials. This act alone deters many impersonators. Yeah, it's intimidating to ask a cop for ID, but as long as you're polite, a real cop won't be obnoxious about it.

If someone seems to have followed you home, don't get out of the car just because you're in your own driveway. You can be attacked there. Stay in the car for a minute; if the follower remains, peel out and head for the cop shop. You might want to get a bottle of pepper spray and Velcro it under the dashboard. (There's more on pepper spray later in this chapter.)

Jogging

Unless you're Deion Sanders, don't count on your speed to protect you. Besides the obvious advice—don't run alone or after dark, leave the Walkman at home—you can consider a few options. Airhorns and mace sprays can be useful, especially since by carrying them you'll feel tougher, and thus look tougher as well. Neither item weighs more than a few ounces. There's no danger of a spray going off accidentally, but make sure you practice, practice, practice. Any target will do—a doll, a chair, an ex-boyfriend. (Okay, don't try the ex-boyfriend at home.) See how far the stream goes. Try the over-the-shoulder squirt for the attacker who's chasing you.

The Walkman prohibition is especially onerous, because lots of us *hate* jogging, and the music is the only thing that makes it bearable. A friend even told me the music makes her feel more confident, which she felt was an even trade-off for the lack of awareness. If you do feel the need for a Walkman, then you have to pay more attention to the other safety factors like time of day, partners, well-traveled paths, and so on.

As for attire, it's not so much what you wear as how you wear it. If you're a bit shy about wearing shorts and scanty tops (do you look at the ground when you pass other people?), then you'll send a signal of vulnerability to any attackers who may be watching you.

Finally, vary your routes and/or the hours you run.

Personal Safety

Over the past few years, the bloom has come off the rose of college safety: We now know that it is a place where date rape and other crimes happen much more than university administrators want to publicize. But even so, college is a much safer place than "the real world," and you must act accordingly. In college, you probably gave everyone the benefit of the doubt; you can no longer do that in the city.

Rule number one: There is no single rule of thumb. When an instructor promises, "This is what to do if you're attacked," beware. That's bull. Each situation is different. No one can definitively state when to run, when to resist, when to submit. So be skeptical of anything you read about this subject. One, there's a lot of lousy information and contradictory advice out there. Two, the data tend to be slanted in some way. For example, studies that use police reports are skewed because they contain the most violent rapes and attacks with weapons (they're most likely to be reported). So take all of the following advice with a grain of salt. You must ultimately use your best judgment.

YELLING

A 1989 UCLA study contended that verbal resistance increases your chances of escape but physical resistance increases your risk of harm. Everyone agrees that verbal defense has no downside. "Stop," "Help," "Police," and "Fire" are commonly advised. I like "Fire" best, because after living in New York for a while, you realize that "Help" might get no reaction from people who don't want to get involved, whereas people like to see where a fire is. "Fire" doesn't work, however, in crowded areas (since people will look around for smoke or flames and assume it's a false alarm). One article suggested yelling, "The man in the red shirt is stealing my purse! Call 911!" But this seems cumbersome to me.

FIGHTING BACK

Leslie Wolfe, director of the Center for Women's Policy Studies in Washington, D.C., has said, "All the research I've seen suggests that learning karate and such is not necessarily learning self-defense. You have to learn how to scream bloody murder. You have to learn how to disobey. But you also have to learn when to recognize that your life's in danger and not to be foolish." Martial arts don't emphasize how to fight on your back using your legs—and that's where most women find themselves during an attack.

People sometimes think, "If I fight back, the attacker might hurt me more." According to Jennie McIntyre of the University of Maryland, the truth is that the attacker's personality, not the level of resistance, determines the extent of injury. Though the evidence is not clear, some studies suggest that the worst injuries happen to women who *don't* fight back, and that those who do fight back can escape a rape up to 80 percent of the time.

While yelling for help is generally considered smart, pleading is not. It just increases an assailant's confidence and power. Some women plead that they are pregnant or threaten that they have AIDS. Some act crazy. Unfortunately, there aren't any statistics on whether these methods work.

SELF-DEFENSE CLASSES

These classes are less about kicking butt than they are about reducing risk in the first place. You may practice with an instructor who wears plastic armor and tries to attack you—this gives you a vague idea of the adrenaline rush you'll feel if you're *really* attacked. You'll learn what it's like to scream, you'll get a chance to spar. More than anything, these practice sessions can help your quality of life; you'll be more relaxed in your day-to-day existence, though there are no guarantees that you can protect yourself.

Many nonprofit groups, rape crisis centers, and local colleges offer classes. Here's what you should look for in a class:

1. Emphasis on prevention and verbal defense.

2. Realistic techniques. A six-step process that culminates in flipping the enemy won't work. K.I.S.S. (Keep It Simple, Stupid) applies here.

3. Instructor's experience. Anybody can be hired to teach a class—he might be an expert, or he might be someone who took a class two years ago and fancies himself an expert. Look for training in self-defense, not in boxing, wrestling, and so on. If you're grabbed, for example, you should learn to stomp on the attacker's insteps, shift your hips, then slam your knee into his groin. That loosens the at-

tacker's grip—at which point you give him a fist to the groin.

4. Learning how to project confidence. A purposeful, upright, steady but quick stride makes you less likely to be attacked. That doesn't mean you should racewalk; just move briskly. Don't look at the ground—some authorities suggest eye contact with passersby, while others advise looking straight ahead.

RANDOM TIPS (ESPECIALLY FOR WOMEN)

- Women should put only their first initial on the mailbox. Also, women might consider having a male friend record the message on their answering machine (even though this might be confusing to prospective boyfriends).
- Confront a would-be assailant. If you're being shadowed, whirl and demand (confidently), "What do you want?" Assertive action frightens away many muggers, according to Jim Bullard of the Memphis police department, who wrote a book called *Looking Forward to Being Attacked*.
- If ordered at gunpoint, should you get into a car? There's no easy answer. According to Bullard, even at knifepoint or gunpoint, do not accede to a command to get into a car. He suggests shouting, "Take my purse, but I'm not going with you"—then running for it. Yet in an article in *Medical Economics* magazine, an expert advises doing whatever an armed assailant says, because any quick move may be construed as an attack.
- When you move to a new apartment, make sure the owner will change the locks. You don't know who lived there before (or two tenants before).
- Some authorities claim that resistance not only provides the best chance of escaping a rape, but also helps reduce the emotional trauma.

- On the elevator with a stranger, stand by the controls. That way you're in better position to hit the Help button.
- On a subway, sit in the car nearest the conductor, or in the middle, where it's least likely to be deserted. On a bus, sit up front. While waiting for the bus, keep your back to the bus stop wall so you can't be taken from behind.
- Keep your door locks well oiled. All you need to do is give them an occasional spritz of WD-40 spray.
- Keep your address and phone number off your checks. If you want to have an address on the check, use a P.O. box.
- Shoulder-strap bags tempt muggers. Backpacks are good because they keep your hands free (wear the straps over both shoulders, even if it does make you look like a nerd). The problem with backpacks, though, is that they leave the little back pocket especially susceptible to being unzipped and looted.
- Don't drop your purse on the front seat of your car when you sit down to drive. Tuck it underneath your seat, so as not to attract a smash-and-grab mugger.
- Approach your car with keys in hand.
- Meet new boyfriends in crowded places, and watch your booze intake.

SELF-DEFENSE SPRAYS

Chemical sprays like Mace can temporarily blind an attacker, while you get away. Some brands also have an ultraviolet dye, which the cops can use to identify an attacker. Yet all of these dyes can be washed off with soap and water, so this limits their efficacy.

Pepper spray, or pepper gas, is an extract of hot pepper—the same stuff you eat at Benny's Burritos. It's not harmful over the long term, and the effects last up to 20 minutes. It can be squirted up to ten feet and costs about $25. Mace is the best-known brand brand name. Call MSI at 800-446-6223 for more information.

There are many disadvantages to sprays. The wind can blow the spray right back at you, blinding you. The mugger can grab the canister and use it against you. Once the mugger has grabbed you, he may be able to hold you powerless in a bear hug, even if you successfully sprayed him and his eyes are shut. The spray also releases adrenaline in the attacker, potentially making him stronger. In some cities and states, pepper gas is illegal; you can be sued for using it, even if you sprayed an actual mugger. Also, you're not supposed to take it on airplanes.

Pepper sprays active ingredient comes in an oil form, which means it must be mixed with alcohol (or another agent) to spray effectively—which, in turn, means it's flammable. Don't keep these sprays in direct sunlight. Glove compartments might also get too hot.

Buying a Spray

Don't buy a pepper gas that's "environmentally friendly"—it won't open the pores enough to be nasty. Don't worry about the percentage of pepper; instead, compare *heat units*, which is how their concentration is measured. An average spray will vary from 500,000 to 1.5 million heat units. Also, look for a flip-top cap and a finger grip, which makes it easier to open, easier to aim, and tougher to grab away from you.

Sprays come in streams and mists. Streams are better in the wind, but mists are more likely to hit the target.

Finally, don't expect too much from pepper gas—like attackers falling to their knees. When you do use it, run like hell and don't stop. You can't expect to stick around and say, "Gotcha!" to an attacker. In one Atlanta case, a woman successfully Maced her attacker in a supermarket parking lot, then did her shopping, came back outside, and was shot dead. With Mace, just as with any self-defense item, you've got to be comfortable using it—which means practice—in order to successfully ward off an attacker.

Household items. Keys and ballpoint pens are always useful in protecting yourself, if you carry them *in your hand* and have them at the ready. Aim for the eye.

Foghorns. These little canisters, about the size of a telephone pager, can emit incredibly loud foghornlike blasts. They're as loud as standing three feet away from a pneumatic drill. They're cheap (a decent one goes for about $30) and can never be used against you. They're legal in every state. You'll have no compunction about using them—whereas you might be reluctant to use Mace if some guy is following you but you can't be sure that he's menacing.

One downside to sirens is that in cities, these personal alarms can blend in with the overall noise. (In New York, false car alarms are so common that no one pays attention anymore.) The other drawback is that these sirens won't help much in desolate areas. Finally, avoid PURSE-ATTACHED SIRENS. The idea is that they'll go off if the bag is yanked. These tend to be ineffective.

Stun guns. This is a bunch of metal contacts on a hand-held device that shoots electric current. It hurts a lot; the jolts run around 100,000 volts. One problem is that you need to get close to the attacker, since the stun gun has a short range. Another is that criminals have various tolerances to pain. If he's not incapacitated, a stun gun will just enrage him. Anecdotal evidence suggests that these devices are not particularly practical. Cheap ones are not worth anything, since they won't deliver enough juice to immobilize. Even good ones seem to be more of a deterrent than a way to stop action against you—and the deterrent works only if the mugger recognizes what the hell you're holding. Stun Tech (800-345-7886) sells them for about $115.

HIGH-TECH PRODUCTS IN THE NEXT TEN YEARS:

- Thermal guns. They work like a microwave, heating up the target.
- Lasers. These will blind the assailant.
- Chemical agents. There is a foam, for example, which is sprayed on the attacker, and when it makes contact, it expands to form a huge glob of goo. This has been used by government agencies for years and will one day come on the market. The goo makes it hard to escape.
- Nets. Dispensed from handheld canisters, these will be sprayed to capture attackers, like *Spiderman*.

Basic First Aid

Now that you're on your own, now that Mom and Dad are gone, now that the RAs and sorority mothers and the school nurse are history, you've got to get a basic first-aid kit. You'll probably accumulate most of the following items anyway, but if you plan ahead and buy them now, you'll save yourself from limping to the drugstore when your mountain-biking excursion takes a turn for the worse.

WHAT YOU NEED

1. **Assorted bandages.** Make sure you include some big gauze squares, Band-Aids (don't go for the no-frills brands here; they don't stick), tape, and an Ace bandage to wrap everything.

2. **A plastic "ice pack."** They're so much easier than filling a towel with ice cubes, then trying to balance it on your bruised shin.

3. **Scissors.** Because *nobody,* not even Mike Tyson, can tear that white adhesive tape.

4. **Pain killer.** There are three basic kinds: aspirin (Bayer), acetaminophen (Tylenol), and ibuprofen (Advil). Aspirin has a potentially useful bonus effect—it thins the blood; is easier on some stomachs; and ibuprofen seems to help most with general body aches.

5. **Sundries.** These should include tweezers, a thermometer, hydrogen peroxide, bacitracin, antacids, laxatives, and anti-diarrhea agent (such as Kaopectate).

6. **First-aid manual.**

TREATING BITES

Whether it's animal or human, Rover from next door or an angry customer, here's the plan.

1. Control the bleeding, if necessary, by applying direct pressure to a gauze pad covering the wound. The trick is, if the blood soaks through the gauze, don't remove it. Instead, apply another compress *on top of* the first.

2. Check for hives, swelling of the mouth, coughing or sneezing, or shortness of breath. Any of these might indicate an allergy. A bee sting, for example, is no big deal for most people, but if you're allergic to bees, you might need to be hospitalized.

3. Wash the wound with warm soap and water for at least five minutes.

4. *Do not* apply any medicines.

5. Use those bandages.

6. Call the doctor.

SNAKE BITES

Snake bites are a special case. Obviously, you need to get to a doctor. If one is not readily available, however, you might need to treat the bite yourself.

1. Don't walk. Don't even move the bitten area (often the leg). Keep still. Look at the bite. A poisonous snake has two Dracula-like fangs; nonpoisonous snakes do not. Therefore, a poisonous bite will look like an upside-down U with two dots above it. A nonpoisonous bite will just look like the upside-down U, without any dots.

2. If the bite is nonpoisonous, skip to step 5.

3. If the bite is poisonous, keep the injured area below heart level, and tie a string (a shoelace will work well) about three inches above the wound. For example, if the wrist is bitten, tie the string onto the forearm; if the ankle is bitten, tie the string onto the shin. This is not to be tied supertight; you're just slowing blood circulation down, not applying a tourniquet.

4. Now things get really dicey. Clean the wound with alcohol. Then sterilize a knife or razor blade. Make a couple of shallow, parallel, vertical incisions about one centimeter over each fang mark—no crisscrosses and no deep cuts, just shallow, vertical incisions. Then you (or someone else) must suck out the blood (assuming you don't have any open sores on your mouth). Suck, spit, suck, spit (don't swallow), for about 30 minutes. If the swelling reaches the first string, leave it but tie a second string three inches above the first. Wash the wound when you're done sucking.

5. Apply a cold compress to the bite (which means a cold, damp cloth). Do *not* pack it in ice.

BLISTERS

1. If the skin is broken, wash it with soap and warm water, blot it dry with a sterile pad, then bandage it. Avoid strong antiseptics and certainly rubbing alcohol; John Wayne may have poured bourbon all over his wounds, but you shouldn't. Use bacitracin ointment instead.

2. If the skin is not broken, *don't break it.* Now you can use rubbing alcohol (to help absorb the liquid buildup underneath the skin), then cover the blister with a protective bandage.

3. If the skin is not yet broken but you think it will break accidentally, wash it, sterilize a needle (by boiling it in water for several minutes), then puncture the blister at its base. Allow the gunk to drain out. Cover it with a pad. You should probably have a tetanus shot ASAP if you puncture a giant blister; that's the kind of thing that can easily become infected.

BRUISES

1. Apply ice quickly.

2. Elevate the bruised area.

3. Take aspirin (that is, not Tylenol or Advil). The blood-thinning effects will help reduce swelling.

BURNS

1. Run the skin under cold water, or apply ice packs.

2. *Do not* apply ointments or salves; the skin needs to breathe.

DIARRHEA

1. Consume clear, liquid foods, like water, broth, and so on.

2. If its's black or bloody, you might be in serious trouble. Go to the emergency room.

INSECT ATTACKS

1. Pull out the stinger gently. If you squeeze too hard, you may force more poison into the skin.

2. For bee stings or mosquito bites, apply baking powder or some other base.

3. For wasp stings, apply lemon juice, vinegar, or some other acid.

4. Apply ice (for either sting).

5. For ticks, if they've already bonded with you, don't try to pull them off. Cover them with motor oil. This often kills them instantly. If not, leave the oil on for a half hour, then wash it off with soap and water. Of course it's best to pull the ticks off before they actually attach to your skin. Just be sure you don't leave any part of the tick, especially the head.

NASTY PLANTS

To treat exposure to poisonous plants, flood the exposed skin with water for at least fifteen minutes. Use soap. Drink lots of water.

chapter ten

Chow: Nutritional Realities

You're not going to believe this. I didn't, not at first. But healthy eating is simple. It may be difficult to *do,* but it's easy to understand.

But you're no dummy, right? You're already suspicious of the magazines in the grocery store checkout line—the grapefruit diets, and "lose ten pounds in ten days!" plans, the fat-free recipes, blah, blah, blah. You pay no attention to those "counselors to the stars," touting their so-called weight-loss achievements on *Sally Jessy* and the rest of the talk-show circuit. You smile at your pal who swears on Kurt Cobain's grave that ginseng or some "alpha potion" or spider extract helps her fight off sickness.

You know this stuff is bogus.

Good. But you might not know that many of the pop nutritionists who appear on the news, who have columns in newspapers, who write best-sellers, who have seemingly advanced degrees are often frauds as well. In other words, even if you steer clear of the obvious morons buying infomercial time, you are still bombarded by pseudoscientists—a step above quacks—armed with nutritional half-truths. Unlike the charlatans of a hundred years ago, who traveled from town to town selling miracle potions, today's "health" vendors have a cloak of respectability. They use ten-dollar scientific words, like *detoxify*, that are meaningless. Usually their "degrees" are certificates that cost $50 and require no exams whatsoever, just a name, address, and of course, a check.

Though health food salespeople, homeopathic product pushers and "nutrition counselors" are often considered quaint, they're part of a $25-billion-a-year industry. Despite all the buzz surrounding "elemental curatives" like bee pollen, mega-doses of vitamin C, and algae, none of these has been proven to have significant effects. Legitimate scientific studies have tried to prove the success of these various products, but have failed.

These fad diets or magic powders *can* have a placebo effect: a subhypnotic (there's *my* ten-dollar word) suggestion that makes the patient *believe* the powder works, so it actually does. This is especially true with chronic fatigue syndrome, back pain, and other stress-related ailments. Even legitimate doctors sometimes prescribe sugar pills for neurotic patients (like me). Still, that's no excuse for fraud. Some of these "health food" purveyors know that they're selling worthless products; others actually have convinced themselves that their products work. In any case, these quacks usually push mega-vitamins.

But most doctors agree that vitamin supplements are not the answer, even if your mother thinks otherwise. They don't "combat stress," nor are they "insurance." If 2 mg of vitamin A is the Recommended Daily Allowance, then 6 mg isn't three times better (or any better, for that matter). Also, the "Recommended Daily Allowance" is a confusing notion. It should balance out over a week or two, not every day. So if you have no vitamin C on Monday and two oranges on Tuesday, you're fine. Women, however, should be aware of mineral deficiencies, like iron or folic acid.

Second, beware of anyone selling "hair analysis" or "computer analysis" or any high-tech jargon. No matter what you answer on these computerized quizzes and no matter what your hair is like, the Acme Analysis Company's computer is programmed to tell you to buy (surprise!) lots of Acme products.

Also to avoid: testimonials ("After just six days on Dr. Foster's Worms and Pretzels diet, I'd lost fourteen pounds!"), conspiracy theories ("The medical profession won't let you know about this . . ."), broccoli-only diets (i.e., anything that revolves around one or two foods), and miracle cures. These "miracle" promises are often vaguely worded (for fear of the FDA). They read, "Wouldn't you like to make love all night long?" rather than, "Drink Longman Juice—a secret potion concocted by virile Amazonian woodsmen—and you'll never suffer impotence again." Obviously there are no miracles in nutrition, no short cuts.

If you do decide to take vitamin supplements, don't pay extra money for "natural vitamins." Your body can't disinguish between vitamins extracted from vegetables and factory-made vitamins. And don't buy from practitioners who sell vitamins directly. This is a conflict of interest.

Okay, So What Is Healthy?

If you can't believe most of what you read or hear about nutrition, then how can you find out what you should be eating?

For starters, know this: Nutrition information doesn't change as fast as you are led to believe. Magazines and publishers have a big financial interest in pushing what's "new" about food. So they'll encourage writers to take a minor, though legitimate, research finding and trump it up into a major breakthrough. It seems like every week you see yet another article entitled "The New Skinny on Fatty Foods."

It works. People buy these magazines. But you, the reader, are the victim of information overload. Lettuce provides good skin tone in last month's issue, lettuce causes colon cancer in this month's, and next month lettuce helps prevent Lyme disease. This "Today it's good for you, Tomorrow it's bad for you" nonsense is so frustrating, it's enough to make you inhale a quart of Häagen-Dazs just to calm down.

So. The basics. You grew up with four food groups. The

FDA now has five. In college, you had your own five groups—chips, beer, pizza, cigarettes, and McDonald's—but now it's time to get serious about eating. By your 30s, you'll have settled into habits which will be extremely hard to change.

How to Use the Pyramid

To use the pyramid, the keys are moderation and balance. Again: moderation and balance. That's all.

Try to eat as wide a *variety* of foods as you can, not just from the different food groups, but *within* each group. So if you have french toast for breakfast, have a baked potato at dinner; if you eat oatmeal and an apple today, have Cheerios and a banana tomorrow. Even if you love carrots and eat them all the time—which is fine—you still have to eat other vegetables.

Likewise, you shouldn't get all of your vitamin C from your daily glass of orange juice. Eat tomatoes, raisins, and strawberries, too. That's balance.

"Moderation" confounds most Americans. Everyone knows that you shouldn't eat an entire box of chocolate-chip cookies. What you may not know: too much of a "healthy food" (like five glasses of OJ at breakfast) is just as bad as too little. Watch your portions. Two servings a day of the protein group does not mean a giant burger for lunch and a big steak for dinner; moderation means small portions of meat. Our culture does not value moderation—most grocery stores don't sell packages with just a few ounces of meat, and restaurants generally serve large portions.

So keep in mind that moderation applies to every food, not just to snack foods. Take pasta—in the 1980s, nutritionists explained that it was "fat-free" and good for you—and sales took off. Many people, though, misunderstood. First, pasta does not *contain* fat, but like all carbohydrates it has lots of calories so it can *cause* fat. Second, who eats spaghetti plain? Many people took the fat-free pasta advice as a cue to load up on huge portions of fettuccine alfredo. Then they wondered why they could no longer fit into their bathing suits.

Pyramid Rules

The USDA has seven guidelines that go with its pyramid.

1. Eat a variety of foods.

2. Maintain a desirable weight. Your weight is a combination of genetics, diet, and exercise. Some people (like me) can seemingly eat endless amounts of food and not gain an ounce of fat. Yes, you hate me. But even if you are genetically predisposed to being overweight, that leaves two factors under your control. And as much as we crave shortcuts, you might as well accept right now that there just aren't any. Fad and crash diets have no long-run value, and can cause big-time medical problems, like heart trouble.

3. Make the vegetable/fruit and grain categories more than half of your total caloric intake (55 to 60 percent).

4. Keep fat, saturated fat, and cholesterol to a minimum. There will be more on this later in the chapter.

5. Consume sugar in moderation.

6. Consume salt in moderation.

7. Consume alcohol in moderation. We all got trashed four times a week during our freshman year. Some people are still at it by their senior year. If this is you, shape up now.

Myths

You probably knew all seven of the USDA rules. Now for a few things you might not know.

MYTH: Sugar causes heart disease.

TRUTH: Sugar does not cause heart disease (it *does* contribute to tooth decay). Sugar does not have more calories per ounce than other carbohydrates, like whole-wheat bread. Sugared *products,* however, do tend to be heavy in calories, which of course can lead to obesity—and *that* can cause heart disease. In other words, it's not the sugar in the doughnut that hurts you, it's the fat.

Sugar is empty calories—energy without any nutrients. So the more sugar you eat, the less room in your diet for nutritious food.

MYTH: Brown sugar is better than white sugar.

TRUTH: Brown sugar is white sugar coated with molasses.

MYTH: Honey is better than table sugar.

TRUTH: Honey is simply a mixture of sugars (glucose, sucrose, and so on), and just because bees make it doesn't mean it has any more nutritious value. (Okay, it has a teensy bit of minerals, but nothing worth talking about.)

MYTH: Saccharin (Sweet 'N Low) and aspartame (Equal) are unsafe.

TRUTH: The debate rages on. We don't know. The Centers for Disease Control claims there isn't "evidence of serious, widespread, adverse health consequences" for aspartame, and the American Medical Association supports saccharin.

MYTH: Sugar causes hyperactivity.

TRUTH: There's no evidence to substantiate this, and much evidence to the contrary, such as a study by the National Institute of Mental Health. Movie actress Gloria Swanson (from the film *Sunset Boulevard*) popularized this myth during the fifties with *Sugar Blues,* a best-seller that blamed sugar for all her emotional and medical problems (which were many). In fact, she was just a weirdo.

MYTH: Sugar causes diabetes.

TRUTH: Genes and obesity cause diabetes. Those who *have*

diabetes must control their blood sugar levels, but they didn't *get* diabetes from eating too much sugar.

MYTH: Alcohol is evil.
TRUTH: Alcohol in moderation is no big deal (unless you're pregnant), though, again, the calories are empty. Red wine, in fact, may be beneficial. Just try not to get trashed. Also, a related problem is that you're likely to snack on chips, dip, pizza, and nuts—high-fat products—while drinking.

MYTH: Adding fiber to foods is important.
TRUTH: Not really. The USDA guideline suggest eating more of those foods that contain fiber naturally, not adding fiber to foods that do not contain it.

MYTH: Hangovers can be cured by coffee, vitamin C, hot-and-sour soup, cold showers, or raw eggs.
TRUTH: Hangovers have no easy cure, according to the FDA. None. You can relieve the symptoms with aspirin and antacid, rehydrate with water, and sleep. That's it.

Some research supports the theory that *congeners* affect the severity of hangovers. Congeners are by-products of fermentation that remain in the alcohol. Different types of liquor have various amounts of congeners—in order of least to most, they are vodka, gin, white wine, whiskey, rum, red wine, and brandy. According to this theory, vodka will give you the mildest hangover.

Other drugs affect food habits, too. Pot gives you "the munchies." Heroin can make you crave sweets (since sugar may suppress the withdrawal symptoms). Cocaine withers away your appetite, which can lead to malnutrition. Nicotine speeds up your metabolism; so when you quit smoking, even if you don't eat more, you'll still gain some weight. Of course, you'll probably compound this effect by eating more, since you'll be craving something to offset the former habit.

MYTH: Protein improves athletic performance and aids in weight loss.

TRUTH: Sure, we need protein. But again, the logic of "what is good in moderate amounts must be great in large amounts" is flawed. Most Americans get more than enough protein. Consuming "extra" protein does not help and can hurt: The liver and kidneys may have to work extra-hard to eliminate the toxins they produce when processing protein molecules. Not to mention the fact that meat tends to be expensive.

In fact, high-protein habits require extra water to rid the body of by-products produced when metabolizing proteins. That can lead to dehydration.

MYTH: Amino acid supplements help you get buff, which, in turn, helps you get laid.
TRUTH: There has been research showing that amino acids help fight certain illnesses. But for normal people, these store-bought amino acids will not "increase your muscle mass" or "help you sleep better." A drug called L-tryptophan, for example, is an amino acid that was marketed as a drug that could help you fall asleep. Before it was taken off the shelves in 1990, this drug was linked with about 1,000 cases of a serious disorder called eosinophilia myalagia. I'll admit I have no idea what that disease is (it sounds scary), if you'll admit you've been tempted to buy these amino acid products. Don't.

MYTH: Raw eggs and raw meat build muscles.
TRUTH: In fact, cooking denatures protein, which makes it more digestible, thus better enabling your body to create muscle tissue. The only upside is that eating raw meat would necessarily exclude the possibility that it was cooked in oil—and too much oil can be a problem. But rawness provides no health benefits and makes food poisoning much more likely.

MYTH: Only meat and fish provide protein.
TRUTH: Almost every culture has some sort of common vegetable protein. Mexicans have pinto beans; Indians have lentils; Lebanese have chickpeas; Japanese have tofu; and Americans

have baked beans, peanut butter sandwiches, and so on. Vegetable protein is a cheaper, healthier way to obtain protein.

MYTH: Ketogenic diets are great for weight loss because they replace high-calorie carbohydrates with low-calorie proteins.
TRUTH: These diets are *very* popular. If you eliminate carbohydrates from your diet for several days, your body will burn fatty acids to create *ketones*. But you don't lose fat. You burn fatty acids, which are not the same as fat. Instead, you have dramatic weight loss—of water. The kidneys are trying to rid the body of excess ketones, so they flush out more water than normal as urine. The moment you return to carbohydrates, you'll regain that water. Ketogenic diets cause headaches, fatigue, even bad breath! (They make the blood more acidic.)

MYTH: Starchy foods are fattening.
TRUTH: Actually, potatoes, bread, bagels, and noodles have the same number of calories per ounce as protein. A six-ounce baked potato has roughly the same amount of calories as a six-ounce piece of flounder. Sure, if you fry the potato, or add a dollop of sour cream, or drown it in butter, it's fattening.

MYTH: Doctors say that about 30 percent of what you eat can be fat.
TRUTH: The American Heart Association recommends that no more than 30 percent of *calories* be fat. But fat has, gram for gram, at least double the calories of carbohydrates or pasta. In fact, *one* ounce of chocolate has around 200 calories—the same as *five* ounces of skinless chicken breast.

MYTH: "Light" margarine is better than the regular kind.
TRUTH: Margarine (and butter, too) is not pure fat; it's about four-fifths fat and one-fifth water. "Light" margarine just means the company added more water (or air), not that they somehow extracted fat from the oil itself. So if you compensate for the taste by putting more "light" margarine on your toast than your usual amount of "regular" margarine, you'll end up with the

same amount of fat. Incidentally, butter may have the same calories per ounce as margarine, but it has more cholesterol.

MYTH: Greasy foods and chocolate lead to pimples.
TRUTH: So far, medical experts believe acne is related to stress and hormone changes. (However, if you do eat lots of high-fat foods and gain weight as a result, you might become stressed out, which *then* results in acne.)

Fats

Fats are confusing. There's saturated and unsaturated, lean and extra-lean, and different types of cholesterols. What's what?

- **Saturated fat** is hard at room temperature. Beef fat, lard, butter, and tropical oils (like coconut oil) fall into this category. That is, they have the highest concentrations of saturated fats. (Each type of oil has at least a little bit of all three types of fat.)
- **Polyunsaturated fat** includes liquid cooking oils like corn oil, safflower oil, and sunflower oil.
- **Monosaturated fat** includes canola oil, olive oil, and Crisco.

Generally, you probably eat too much fat and want to reduce all three types.

The actual difference among these three fats is not important (each type of fat molecule has a different number of hydrogen atoms). Saturated fat is the one most associated with high blood cholesterol, although that's not completely understood by scientists. Monosaturated fat (like olive oil) is generally less harmful than polyunsaturated fat (like corn oil), which is generally less harmful than saturated fat (like butter). But even this is tricky: Crisco is monosaturated, but if you eat it your body creates *trans fatty acids,* which *act* very much like saturated fats.

Confusing? Of course. Just keep them all to a minimum

and know that all three kinds of fat have about nine calories per gram. So if you're one of those people who have the time and desire to keep track of fat intake, your limit is about 600 to 700 calories of fat per day (out of a total diet of 2,200 calories per day). That translates to about 65 to 75 *grams* of fat per day. Remember that foods that are low in *fat*—like pasta—may be high in *calories*, and vice versa.

Fish Fat

Everyone knows that fish is good for you. But did you know that fish varies in fat content? Flounder has less than one-tenth the fat per ounce of shad. Salmon has nine times more fat than haddock. Generally, the darker the fish (mackerel, albacore tuna), the higher the fat content. Still, no matter what the fish, it still has less fat than red meat.

Cholesterol

Cholesterol isn't always bad. There are two basic kinds: *dietary*, which is cholesterol in the food you eat, and *serum*, which is cholesterol in your blood. This is confusing, so again, the cholesterol that you eat is not the same as the cholesterol in your blood.

You should be more worried about the serum cholesterol, the kind in your body. This kind not only comes from your diet, but is also manufactured by your body. In other words, you might not *eat* foods with high (dietary) cholesterol, yet could still have high *serum* cholesterol. It's tricky stuff.

Your body makes roughly 1,000 mg of serum cholesterol per day. About 100 mg of this circulates in your blood. The rest sits in cells, nerves, and so on. There are two types of this serum cholesterol: *LDL* and *HDL*. LDL is the "bad" kind; HDL is the "good" kind. Note that this has nothing to do with dietary cholesterol. Your goal is to keep a good *proportion* of HDL to LDL, and to keep the *overall level* of cholesterol (that is, both types combined) below 180 mg per deciliter.

So what the hell does that mean?

Being a lazy, snack-attack-prone couch potato lowers the HDL levels. Got that? Bad habits like overeating and not exercising can actually *lower* cholesterol levels. The problem is, they lower the "good" cholesterol—the HDL. In turn, that leaves only the LDL—the "bad" cholesterol—which ultimately means that your proportion of HDL to LDL is out of whack. Meanwhile, the juicy T-bone you're eating will ultimately raise your LDL level.

The bottom line is that you have two serum cholesterol concerns: the overall amount, and the balance of HDL to LDL.

BOOZE AND CHOLESTEROL

Alcohol, ironically, raises the HDL, or "good" cholesterol, levels (which is why some studies suggest that a daily glass of wine helps diminish the chance of heart disease). But alcohol creates other problems, so it's not a smart way to get your serum cholesterol under control.

CUTTING YOUR CHOLESTEROL

This subject is still not understood. Most doctors, however, would agree with these tips:

1. Reduce your consumption of egg yolks and fatty red meats. When you do eat meat, trim away visible fat, and drain it when cooking. Lean red meat, however, has no more cholesterol than chicken or fish. Also, most restaurants offer egg-white omelettes, so if the taste doesn't bother you too much, eat 'em.

2. For your meat-free dinners, don't give back all your health gains by using lots of cheeses and heavy sauces.

3. The margarine that comes in tubs is better than the sticks, since tub margarine is usually whipped with air. Just don't use any more tub margarine than your would stick margarine, or the benefit is lost.

4. Don't look at the "cholesterol-free" advertisements. Read the *label*—that's where the truth is. On the label, look to avoid coconut and palm oils, animal shortening, and "partially hydrogenated vegetable oils."

5. Eat beans, apples, and other high-fiber foods.

6. Most steaks and meats are cut in packages too large for one person. Instead of buying the prepared meats, get the butcher to chop you smaller portions, and have him trim the fat while he's at it.

One more thing: The way your body deals with cholesterol is partially hereditary. Some people could feast on Ore-Ida products every day and not have cholesterol problems; others are at risk even if they never so much as glance at an egg. Ask your folks if they have cholesterol problems.

How to Eat Out

First things first: All-you-can-eat deals, like the HoJo fish fry, are killers. Not only is the temptation to eat seven servings of fried flounder impossible to resist, but the gluttonous atmosphere makes you want to gorge to get your money's worth. When you are faced with a buffet, start with salad. That'll make you start to feel full by the time you're ready to attack the rest of the offerings. Eat slowly, too. It takes 20 minutes or so for your body to register that you are "full."

A lot of magazine articles about nutrition expect you to eat perfectly healthy meals in restaurants, like the "vegetable platter" and fresh fruit for dessert. Well, what the hell is the point of eating out if you're stuck with boring food? Let's be realistic.

The key is to make *trade-offs*. If you want to have french fries, then skip the dressing on your salad. If you want to have a dessert, then skip the beer.

RESTAURANT 101

- Beware the bread basket. Have everyone at the table take one roll, then ask your companions if it's okay for the waiter to get the basket off the table. Otherwise, you'll chow on it, then feel obligated to stuff yourself with the main course—since that's what you paid for in the first place—even though you're about to explode from the nine dinner rolls.

- Start with a salad or light soup (like chicken noodle or vegetable, not cream of broccoli or french onion). That will fill you up a bit and help you avoid devouring the steak you ordered.

- Have the waitress ask the chef to make you a small portion. Some restaurants make this easy. Red Lobster offers lunch and dinner portions of fish; my folks always order the smaller, cheaper lunch portions, even at dinnertime. This sometimes ticks off the waiter (he has a smaller check, which means a smaller tip), but the portions always seem to be enough to satisfy. Even though most often you're paying for the full-sized meal when you ask for a smaller cut, you're better off. Otherwise, you'll likely eat whatever's on your plate, even if it's more than you actually want.

- When you're finished but there's still food on the plate, ask the waitress to clear it (and take a doggie bag if you wish). Otherwise, you'll nibble while you chat.

- Sauces can be fat traps, especially hollandaise, bearnaise, and other French varieties. Do a Meg Ryan (as in, *Harry and Sally*)—ask for it on the side.

- Japanese food tends to be low in fat, though high in sodium.

- Even though some people find it embarrassing, ask to

share a dinner. If you're still hungry, you can always order an appetizer afterwards.

- Some nutritionists tell you to order salads instead of burgers at fast-food restaurants. Puh-leeze. What you can do, again, is make trade-offs. If you're craving the Big Mac (or, as Travolta would say, "le Royale"), fine—but trade the shake for a Sprite. If you really want a quarter-pound Roy Roaster, go for it—but have a baked potato with just salt and pepper (1 gram of fat) instead of a biscuit (21 grams of fat). At Pizza Hut, enjoy a large pie, but choose mushrooms as your topping (30 calories per pie, assuming they're not fried) instead of pepperoni (557 calories).

On Vegetarianism

More and more people are becoming vegetarians. Is vegetarianism healthy?

It depends. There are three basic levels of vegetarians. Some avoid red meat—that's generally good. Others also avoid chicken, fish and eggs—which can increase protein and iron problems. A third group avoids all of these *and* won't eat dairy products—in other words, nothing that comes from an animal. This last group are called vegans, and account for only about 2 percent of vegetarians.

Whether vegetarianism leads to better health is still debatable. Seventh-Day Adventists, for example, have low rates of heart disease. They don't eat meat. They also don't smoke or drink. Mormons avoid booze and cigarettes, too, but they eat meat. Mormans have similarly low rates of heart disease. Both groups, too, emphasize low-stress, traditional lifestyles, which probably contributes to their health as well.

Still, most authorities agree that vegetarians make some great health gains: they're less likely to be fat, and they have lower blood pressure and fewer stomach problems. The downsides, though, can include iron deficiencies, since plant iron is much harder to absorb than animal iron; also, calcium and vitamins D, B_{12} and B_2 may be lacking. While vitamin D can be gained from sunshine and vitamin B_2 from nuts, it's harder to get enough B_{12} or calcium without non-plant foods. If you're a vegetarian, it's probably smart to use vitamin supplements, though you should ask your doctor.

Diets That Work

Is this you:

On December 26th, you commit yourself to an ambitious diet and exercise regime for the new year. On January 1, you make a special exception, staying in bed until 2 P.M. with a hangover, then settling into the couch with chips and a remote for the bowl games. But true to your word, you eat right and jog a few laps for the next three days. On January 5th you're super-busy at work, so you skip the running and are forced to skip lunch and grab a Double Whopper with Cheese later that afternoon. On January 6th you're back on track, but the next day your boss yells at you, so you comfort yourself with a quarter-pound Hershey bar. Then you feel too full to jog. Over the next few days, you struggle to hang on, but finally submit to failure. Another year wasted.

If this is you, then don't worry: It means you're a human being. Some people stick to their very first effort at solid nutrition and exercise; these people should be shot. The rest of us struggle mightily and fail often.

Three Rules for Dieting

Step one to changing your behavior is accepting that it's *really* hard. The changes must be long-term. That means every single one of those six-day diets in *Cosmopolitan* or similar magazines is probably a farce.

The difficult task of making a long-term change is only

compounded by our age. It's hard to imagine being 60 with heart disease, yet so easy to eat another can of Pringles. We all sort of plan to begin healthy eating in our 30s, when we have kids. But by then, your eating habits will be so ingrained into your personal culture, they'll be tough to amend.

Step two is the change itself. Almost anybody can keep this up for a day or two, or even a week. Exercise more. Eat less. Both in moderation.

Step three is the hard part: changing how you respond to various impulses. Often boredom and depression trigger overeating, and there's no easy answer. If you're bored at work, you may not be able to switch jobs easily. If you're depressed over not having a girlfriend or boyfriend, it's not as if you can remedy the situation overnight. But even if you can't force the issue of companionship, you can take action to increase your self-esteem (volunteerism, in my opinion, is the best way).

Step three also involves your social eating habits. This change is hard to accomplish on your own, and if you can find friends with good habits (or at least a similar commitment to developing good habits), your life will be a lot easier. Meanwhile, if "the boys" head out to KFC a couple of times a week, you're going to have a tough time ordering a salad, what with that fried-chicken aroma and all the razzing you'll have to endure. The KFC trip is probably a situation you have to avoid, which may mean a big social sacrifice. You may decide that nutrition isn't worth it.

The bottom line is that the *only* smart, healthy way to shed poundage is simply to work out and eat a smaller but well-proportioned diet. Totally boring, yes, but it's the only way.

Fad Diets

- **Ketogenic diets.** These low carbohydrate/high protein diets are discussed in the Myths section of this chapter. You'll end up with excessive fat and protein in your diet, and the omission of any food group is a mistake.

- **Fruit and fruit juice only.** These are the worst types of diets; they can cause low blood pressure, shock, and even death.
- **Repetitious diets.** These are based on the true principle that you'll lose weight it you eat the same foods every day. Why? Because you'll be bored and eat less than your hunger dictates.
- **Preloading.** Eating bran or drinking water before meals does, of course, decrease your appetite. But preloading is usually combined with one of these other fads—it's obviously not the water that's a problem, it's tricking yourself into thinking that you're full so you'll be satisfied with just a lonely grapefruit for dinner.
- **Two weeks on/two weeks off.** These diets emphasize low carbohydrates and no milk. They're not awful, but again, restricting food groups is problematic.
- **Macrobiotic diets.** These endorse eliminating various foods, one at a time, starting with desserts, then meats, then fruits, then soups, until all that's left are grains and a bit of tea and water. These Zen diets are dangerous.
- **Powdered shake mixes.** Just because they have protein and vitamins does not mean your body's need for *food* with protein and vitamins is replaced.
- **"Timing" diets.** There's no scientific evidence to show that you can lose weight by eating at certain times of the day.
- **Also avoid:** appetite suppressants, starch blockers, diuretics, body wraps, and the like.

A Few Final Words

Changes in your lifestyle can offer big nutritional opportunities—or dangers. If you date or marry someone with good habits, it will inevitably rub off on you. Finding yourself unemployed, on the other hand, is often so frustrating that the free time will have you chowing away.

Leaving college and entering the workplace has a profound impact on your diet. Now that you have a job, you skip breakfast (no time) then snack or drink coffee to make it till noon. You order lunch at your desk and gulp it down or go out for fast food (no time to pack a lunch). You eat dinner alone while reading the paper or watching the news, either rushing through the meal (bad for digestion) or overeating (distracted by Peter Jennings).

The soundest advice is simple (you've already heard it a million times), but it's worth repeating. One, drink lots of water—not soda, not iced tea, not lemonade—throughout the day. Two, breakfast like a king, lunch like a prince, dinner like a pauper. The rationale is two-fold. Your body functions best when all digestion is completed before bedtime. Also, breakfast and lunch items tend to be less expensive.

BREAKFAST

Breakfast should be a slow, large meal, but *not* the big, greasy, bacon-and-egg deal. If you're willing to take the time to prepare and eat a big breakfast, experiment with eating "dinner foods," like chicken, fish, or a salad. If you're going to stick with regular breakfast foods, then milk, fruit, and juice are all solid elements. Now is the time to give up cold cereals that (a) you've seen advertised on Saturday morning cartoons, or (b) are deliberately misspelled (such as Cap'n Crunch). Doughnuts have a lot of fat. Croissants are made with tons of butter. Bagels are fine, but watch out for the cream cheese smothering. Avoid high-sugar muffins that taste suspiciously like cake—because that's exactly what they are.

LUNCH

Take a 20-minute walk before lunch. This will relax you and help digestion. Don't eat while you work; you'll be less productive overall, even with the extra hour of desk time. If you have time, pack your lunch: It's not only cheaper, but if you make it after breakfast (that is, when you're full), you won't overeat.

DINNER

Cooking for one is a bummer. Still, without going cookbook on you, here are three thoughts if you're willing to do more than nuke a burrito and boil some spaghetti.

1. Olive oil is a chef's best friend. Whether you're simply frying up an omelette, sautéing some 'shrooms, or sizzling a cod filet, olive oil will add something to your dish. For example, instead of pouring Ragu all over your spaghetti, spend fifteen minutes chopping and frying bell peppers, onions, fresh tomatoes, zucchini, and fresh garlic in a pan of olive oil. A hint: Crumble up spices into an *empty* skillet—whether sage, rosemary, thyme, pepper, whatever—and heat the spices for a minute by themselves. This releases their flavor. Only then add the olive oil.

2. Fish is particularly nutritious and hard to screw up as long as it's fresh (buy it the same day you'll eat it). If it's a bit undercooked or a bit overdone, it's not a big deal—certainly not compared to say, chicken, which can make you very sick if it's too raw or become extremely dry if it's too well done. To cook any fileted light-colored fish—flounder, haddock, cod, turbot, roughy, and the like—simply throw on a lump of butter, a little salt and pepper, and maybe some paprika or garlic, and shove it in the broiler. After a few minutes, squeeze a lemon onto it. *Voilà.*

3. If you find yourself buying take-out every day, experiment with a hybrid of part take-out, part make-it-yourself. For example, there's nothing easier than cooking a steak: Buy a beauty for $5 at the grocery store and throw it into the broiler; cut it open at the middle to see when it's done. Rather than hustling over a side dish, you can pick up a hot spinach-and-rice as you walk home from the grocery for another $2. For the same price as Chinese food loaded with MSG and without an ounce more of your own sweat, you get a legitimate tasty dinner to savor at home.

Epilogue

1. Always send hand-written thank-you notes.
2. Never skimp on toilet paper or champagne.
3. Garlic is good.